# Acknowledgements

This book is a combination of knowledge, experience and skills from various sources but, most of all, from the material diligently gathered by Principal Stewart Liddle between 1951 and 1968. I would like to thank Principal Janet Lowe for having the confidence in my abilities to take on such an important and responsible project, and for her help and guidance throughout the project and Tom Dodds, Assistant Principal, for his help and encouragement. I am grateful to Derrick Barclay, Curator of the Andrew Carnegie Birthplace Museum, Chris Neale of the Dunfermline Library, and numerous Lauder College staff, past and present, for their help and understanding, and people of Fife who gave me first hand knowledge and advice on the history of this remarkable College on its 100th Anniversary.

Particular thanks are due to the Trustees and staff of the Carnegie Dunfermline Trust and the staff of the Dunfermline Library, the Dunfermline Press and the Carnegie Birthplace Museum.

Special thanks to Marianne Philp for excellent word processing services and patience through many drafts.

With grateful thanks to Clydesdale Bank PLC and Babcock Rosyth Defence Ltd for providing generous financial assistance with the publication of this book.

Dominic J Currie
April 1999

# Note from the Principal

As Lauder College approached its Centenary Year, I invited Dominic J. Currie to research and write The Lauder Legacy as a contribution to the celebrations.

I am pleased to support and endorse the publication of the book, on behalf of Lauder College, and to commend the author for his diligence and determination to bring to life the College's history and the legacy of its founder, George Lauder.

The Lauder Legacy does not pretend to be a fully comprehensive historical work. Such a project was beyond our resources. It aims to convey a flavour of the life and times of George Lauder and Lauder College through highlights and examples carefully selected from a range of source material by the author, from his own unique perspective.

Dominic and I are aware that much detail and many characters have not found space on these pages. We apologise unreservedly for any omissions or inaccuracies and trust that no offence will be taken, as none is intended.

We hope that readers of the Lauder Legacy will enjoy and value it, in the spirit in which it was written.

Janet Lowe
Principal of Lauder College
April 1999

# Foreword

*As the great, great, grandson of George Lauder, and on behalf of his other descendants all of whom live in the United States, I wish to convey the great pride we all feel on the occasion of the Centenary of Lauder College and the publication of this history of the family and the development of the College.*

The following pages include a description of the growth of George Lauder from a boy of humble circumstances into a prominent citizen of Dunfermline with his far-sighted and strong advocacy of practical education. They also include an account of the Lauder and Carnegie families, their intermarriage and enduring, close relationship, setting the scene for George Lauder's intercession with his beloved nephew, Andrew Carnegie, and the founding of the College one hundred years ago.

The author then presents a detailed and interesting history of the growth of Lauder College from its small beginning to its current unique and important position among the educational institutions of Scotland. It is an engrossing story, well told.

How astonished and proud George Lauder would be if he could see the College that bears his name and how much he would appreciate the efforts of all those involved in its successful development over the past century.

We, George Lauder's descendants, are delighted that our ancestor's vision has been so tellingly realized, and, as we know he would, look forward to Lauder College making an ever more important contribution to the lives of those in Dunfermline and the rest of Scotland.

To use one of Lauder College's mottoes: "Briz Yont" (press forward)!


George V Lauder
Washington, DC
2 March 1999

# Contents

George Lauder
1815 - 1901

# Introduction

Dunfermline has every reason to be proud of its contribution to the development of education in Scotland. This contribution, stretching back many centuries, includes primary, secondary, further and higher education as well as social, political and economic education.

The marriage of Malcolm Canmore to Margaret, sister of Edgar Aetheling, in the eleventh century marked an important turning point in the development of education for Fife and Scotland. Margaret brought with her a culture and a passion for learning which sowed the educational seeds for future generations. Margaret's first pupil was the King himself, her husband, whom she taught her own language, instructing him in the art of reading, writing and other equally important subjects, on a formal and technical basis. She also taught the common people, whom she was especially desirous of educating. In this way Scotland's royal residence in Dunfermline became one of the nation's very first centres for education and its influence began to manifest throughout the rest of the country.

Dunfermline's more spectacular contribution, however, has been in the personalities who have distinguished themselves in the advancement of the town and in particular the advancement of education. Of these, no list can be considered complete that omits the names of two of the town's most important sons, George Lauder and Andrew Carnegie. To younger generations of pupils, students and teachers George Lauder is perhaps little more than a name. Those people who belong to older generations of Scottish worthies, like the more famous Andrew Carnegie, who knew the man, and who were privileged to have been associated with him and observed him in the course of his work, will always cherish a high regard for him as one of Scotland's educational pioneers. His devotion to this cause impressed everyone with whom he came into contact.

That he possessed great qualities of ability, courage and honesty was admitted even by his strongest opponents. Even those who opposed his visions for the future bore testament to his tireless energy and struggle for more progressive developments in all aspects of society. The character and forward thinking of George Lauder became an inspiration and a catalyst for numerous developments within and beyond the ancient kingdom of Fife.

His tireless campaign to introduce a proper water system into Dunfermline is legendary, advocating methods which were far in advance of his day and age and refusing to be defeated when faced with large scale setbacks. From 1883 he was a founder member of the local library, serving on its committee for almost ten years and advocating that accommodation be provided in the library for various societies which may well have been the beginning of evening classes, as well as supporting the need for a reference library. He put forward a scheme to provide electric light and power to Dunfermline and argued the advantages and disadvantages of gas, putting forward an elegant compromise which he costed in great detail.

In politics he was a keen radical and he possessed beyond doubt the courage of his convictions. Intensely interested in public affairs he was, alongside his well-known brother-in-law Bailie Thomas Morrison, who was a member of Dunfermline Town Council for more than forty years, a champion of the Chartist cause in Fife. Add to this, Lauder's years as a single parent with a young son to feed support and educate, following the untimely death of his wife, and you have some measure of Lauder the man.

But it was to the cause of education, above all else, that George Lauder was prepared to make great sacrifice in order that its future would be open and relevant to all sections of a hard working and underprivileged society. Free secondary education, and more especially technical education, was seen by Lauder as the most urgent priority in the late nineteenth century. His was a quest to redress the educational balance and to reassess basic educational principles: what was education for? and in what ways should it affect society?

Lauder was born into a Dunfermline which had a reputation for radical thought and militancy. This rapidly growing town was in the forefront of a thriving Scottish industrial economy. A town which, though in transition from the old traditional methods to new revolutionary ways of industry, could still lay proud claim to being famous in an expanding British Empire for its linen.

Lauder's own educational upbringing after 1815 paid more attention to the complexities of his father's snuff mill, the constant clacking of the weaver's shuttle and the street oratory of the local Chartist leaders' demands for justice than any reports of victory at Waterloo or royal shenanigans around an unstable Prince Regent. In an age when formal education was sparse and costly the wealthy could send their children to private schools while the poor had to rely on Sunday and charity schools. Even then poverty and servitude was a common fate for many a good scholar. There was a fear among many of the authorities that educating the poor at all would be bad for the country as well as asking for trouble. One aristocrat was quoted to say: *"It would enable them to read seditious pamphlets, vicious books and publications against Christianity and render them insolent to their superiors."*

Young and older children from poorer families had to be content with an education of sorts gleaned from their peers or from the bitter teacher of experience during a lifetime at the shuttle or down the local coalmine. Those 'learning' days often began at 4 o'clock in the morning working in semi-darkness and filth drawing tubs of coal from a coal face fourteen hours a day, survival being the single subject on the curriculum.

These harsh realities bred quick maturity and for most young men in Dunfermline, including George Lauder, the factories, mills and coalmines still beckoned more than any formal educational opportunity.

George Lauder's progressive crusade brought an entirely fresh vision for secondary education and was directed towards a system of free schooling and the inclusion within the curriculum of some form of technical training.

From as early as 1835 Lauder had supported a visiting Edinburgh lawyer when he had addressed a Dunfermline audience on the subject of "Free Education from School to the University" and for the remainder of the century he kept the aim of free secondary and technical education firmly at the forefront of his campaigns.

It had taken time and hard work in the mid eighteenth century, by people like Lauder, for Scotland to have any real level of devolved authority from England over its educational affairs. The long awaited Education Act of 1872 made scant provision for some schools to add a little extra to the elementary curriculum in 'specific subjects'. However the opinion of most school inspectors was that just tacking bits on to the end of primary schooling was worse than useless. Even when it became evident that a more practical type of training was, in the face of ever increasing foreign competition, vitally necessary, it was decided that it should be industrial training for "masters and managers" only, a far cry from Lauder's plea of training for "every apprentice."

George Lauder was elected onto the Dunfermline School Board in 1876 where he played a key role in many important decisions, mainly regarding elementary education, but it was in matters relating to further and technical education that Lauder displayed his clarity of vision and enthusiasm.

When in 1893 local ratepayers, following a massive campaign of opposition by the School Board, rejected a proposal put forward by Lauder to build a technical school he decided that his cause would be better served by working outside of the School Board and thus he tendered his resignation.

After long and lengthy discussions with his nephew, the millionaire and philanthropist Andrew Carnegie, over a number of years following his resignation from the School Board, George Lauder was at last able to inform the Chairman of the Board in 1897 that he had been authorised "by one who was a true friend to Dunfermline and a well well-wisher of its educational advancement", to say that he (Carnegie) was prepared to lay out a sum of money for the building and supply of a Technical School for the town. For Lauder the opening of a Technical School in 1899 would be a major step in his campaign for free secondary and technical education. For the people of Fife and Scotland, its value, in terms of relevant practical education in tune with an expanding Scottish industry, far outweighed its eventual price. It was to become a flagship of Technical Education in Fife and Scotland.

Like many great undertakings, the beginnings of Lauder College were small and tentative, but having been founded on sound principles, backed by the skills and intelligence of countless staff and students over the past ONE HUNDRED years who have made their own unique contribution to its progress, the College now sits firmly in the 'Cradle of Kings' alongside a host of heroes and institutions as one of the pioneers of enterprise. The College has, through a century of turmoil and change, remained progressive in its ideas, humane in its character, educative in its purpose, dynamic in its operation and continuously inter-woven with communities and industry throughout Fife and beyond.

Lauder Technicial School opened in Priory Lane on 10th October 1899 and provided, in its early years, courses in weaving, electricity, engineering, design, construction and mining for a few hundred students. Today Lauder College's main campus is in Halbeath and the College has annexes in 17 locations across south east and central Scotland from Galashiels to Grangemouth. In 1997-98 14,436 students enrolled to study courses as diverse as childcare and mechatronics.

ONE HUNDRED years on, it would be difficult to find a family in Fife who has not had some connection with Lauder College at some point. Its history has become a history of families - the Lauders, the Carnegies, and the thousands of families in the Scottish communities and industry who have all benefited and contributed in equal measure to the success and development of the College and the Scottish economy.

Its proud and honourable history is second only to the potential it still holds for the numerous generations still to come. Its thrust and energy over the past ONE HUNDRED years have singled it out as having made a unique and dynamic contribution to further and higher education in Fife and Scotland. It is further evidence, if more was needed, of the wisdom and foresight of one of Dunfermline's greatest sons, George Lauder.

*Abbot Patrick, about Ann: 1185.*

As far back as the twelfth century books and reading were an important aspect of life following Margaret Canmore's educational desires. (DPL LHC)

Margaret Canmore had a passion for learning. Here we see her with her first pupil, her husband King Malcolm. She also taught the common people whom she was especially desirous of educating. In this way Scotland's royal residence in Dunfermline became one of the nation's very first centres for education. (DPL LHC)

# George Lauder

On the evening of Sunday 22nd December 1901, Andrew Carnegie, millionaire and philanthropist, sank down at his desk and wrote, in broken tones, to his lifelong friend, cousin Dod after learning of the sudden death of George Lauder, his uncle:

*". . .What this loss is to you and to me no one knows but ourselves; they cannot know. I don't believe there ever was so sweet, so fond an attachment on earth, as there was between us three men - the Teacher and his pupils."*

Heart-broken, Carnegie had very good reason to lament the passing of his Uncle Lauder. Throughout his lifetime he had been his mentor and guide. To Carnegie, George Lauder was everything and more. He was Scotland personified and he was the world in perspective. To the communities of Fife and beyond Lauder had come to symbolise the intense pioneering spirit and character of the new century into which he had led them.

George Lauder was born in the year of hope and storm on 9th May 1815, in the ancient parish of Dunfermline in Scotland at a time when chronic disease, premature ageing and death were common facts of life. He was their only son in a family of five: Isobel (26.3.1811), Marion (25.3.1813), Elizabeth (22.9.1817) and Ann (26.5.1820)

His father, George Lauder husband of Margaret Muir, married in circa 1810, was a snuff miller and had come from a long pedigree of Lauders. Of Norman origin, de' Laueder was mentioned among the barons of the time of Malcolm Canmore and Sir Robert de' Lawedre was a companion in arms to the great Sir William Wallace. At one point in history the ancient Lauders, reputed to have been pirates, owned the Bass Rock and where there is now only ruins, once stood a thriving castle guarding the gateway to the Forth. By 1815, the flag of the skull and crossbones had been replaced by the flag of enterprise when Lauder's father sought to make a living in the snuff trade. The nineteenth century was investing faith and effort into what was euphemistically being called 'progress', meaning mostly material technological advance.

Progress aside, children as young as eight, despite numerous protests, were working for a most unreasonable and cruel length of time daily and any thoughts of abolition were seen as utopian. Even so, it was still a time of much improvement in the general standard of living for many of the 7,000 Dunfermline inhabitants. Brick, stone and tiles were replacing wood, plaster and thatch as common building materials for the 900 dwellings, and cheap cotton made a change of clothes common practice. The growing Industrial Revolution was heralding the best of times and the worst of times in a town:

> *Where village statesmen walk'd with thoughts profound.*
> *And news much older than their beer went round.*

Dunfermline at this time was confined to an area of 900 acres stretching from East Port to Chalmers Street and from Bothwell Street to Golfdrum. Few houses in those days had piped water and most of the inhabitants had to carry their quota in buckets to the home from public wells. Lauder was too young to remember the excitement which roused the Scottish nation when the remains of King Robert the Bruce were accidentally unearthed in February 1818, but may have been old enough to have had some childish recollections of the King's re-interment in Dunfermline Abbey in November 1819.

Lauder's formal schooling remains a mystery, but less of a mystery perhaps was the powerful educational influence of his father and the beautiful surroundings of his modest size snuff mill in the 'Glen' which formed part of Pittencrieff estate. The mill was just a stone's throw from 'The Abbey' which held the remains of King Robert the Bruce, from where a steep decline formed part of the 'Tower Burn' which ran under the ruined windows of 'The Palace', where Charles I was born. This burn had been put to good use by the earlier inhabitants of Dunfermline who had constructed a dam and led water by a lade to provide the necessary power to operate three mills at the top end of what is now appropriately known as Bruce Street: a Flour Mill, which had the first use of the water, then parted with it to a Meal Mill, whose tail race finally fed the wheel of the lowest, Lauder's Snuff Mill. Here an indelible impression was created on the senses of young Lauder who was always listening and always learning.

The tall trees rising from the Glen had their tops stirred by the winds of the upper world, whilst in the lower and darker world to which they gave protection, there was scarcely enough breeze for the millers of the upper two mills to winnow their grain. There was a perpetual sound of splashing water as it whirled the large wooden wheels amid the clatter and grind of the machinery as it did its work. When young Lauder made his first assisted descent from one level to the other by the steep access steps, he would have been met by the aroma of wheat flour, then of oatmeal, and finally, amidst the odour of adjacent undergrowth and leaf mould, the heavy fragrance of tobacco and perfumes blending together to make the snuff. The sights, sounds, smells and cool feel of the water spray were so different from the familiar domestic scene that they made the experience unforgettable and the adventure one to be remembered.

So the young George Lauder, as he grew to boyhood, found his way many times to the old snuff mill and, like little 'Hiawatha', learned many things.
The emptying of the hogsheads, the chopping and batching of the tobacco midribs and leaves, the long fermentation process, the grinding between the big granite stones and in the large conical iron mortars with their wooden linings, the riddling, the moistening, the blending and the 'doctoring' to give each kind its characteristic "flavour" and the packaging for despatch to the merchants, local shopkeepers and individuals. With all these processes, as a matter of course, he became technically and studiously acquainted and took none of them for granted. Through the most natural of processes, Lauder absorbed the practical geography and pharmacognosy of the various tobaccos, and spices such as clove and cinnamon, essential oils such as lavender and peppermint, bitter almonds and tonquin beans, bergamot and Attar of Roses.

In time, thanks to the indulgence of his father and the good nature of the millers, young Lauder gave some general assistance with the processes and in running an occasional errand, but his greatest joy was in the workshop, a necessary adjunct designed to render the mill as self-sufficient as possible in the important matters of maintenance and packaging.

The workshop was equipped with the minimum working tools of the engineer and, because the wheel-buckets were of wood, the grinding mortars timberlined, and the crates required to be repaired or 'made-down', woodworking tools were an essential part of the workshop. Here the boy revelled and, whenever the workshop was temporarily vacant, numerous boyish treasures flowed from his busy hands. The other millers, recognising his youthful enthusiasm, were always keen to help him over the more difficult phases and would correct him if any clumsy use of the tools endangered his fingers. As he grew older and his tastes changed and he became more dexterous with the tools, he would undertake to help with more serious tasks.

From the millers and other workers he would learn much besides, especially at times when they sat down for their 'piece break' and the air broke out with conversation. Much of what they said may have passed over young Lauder's head but when the conversation became animated or laughter rang out or tempers were frayed, there was Lauder in the background always listening and always learning. The rights of the snuff mill to the water of the lade, in view of the higher situation of the other two mills, was often fiercely debated with the same passion as the 'rights of man'. Recalled with glee was the story of how, many years before, the weavers of Dunfermline decided that they needed a common bleachfield and had found a place to suit in the King's Park, (later 'Abbey Park') which, being just to the west of the Heuch, was conveniently near to the town centre and the sun, and had water already provided through the proximity of the Heuch Mills lade. All they needed to do, it seemed, was to persuade the proprietor, who happened to be the Flour Miller, to let them have it. This, however, he resolutely refused to do. Whereupon the weavers, inspired by their Deacon, one David Morrison (note the name), decided to become teetotal until the miller realised the error of his ways. Since the Flour Miller was a maltster as well as a miller, this heroic act of self-denial by the weavers hit his pocket so hard that he was eventually reduced to consenting to 'give up his tack', and the weavers secured their bleachfield as they had planned, and Lauder listened and learned.

From time to time a miller would bring in a newspaper, a scarce commodity then, and this would be read aloud to the circle of men by he who had the ability. This would be another source of education for young George Lauder as the working men of Dunfermline in the early 1800s were intelligent and critical, politically well informed and active.

It would have seemed natural for George Lauder to have followed in his father's footsteps, becoming his partner at the mill but this was not to be.

The snuff-taking habit, after more than a century of growth, had passed its peak. New habits were being formed with the introduction of the 'paper cigar' (cigarette) and this was taking the place of the older product for many people. Around 1827 snuff milling was fast becoming a declining industry, so Lauder chose handloom weaving instead. Of all the skilled craftsmen in the town, two out of every three were weavers, producing table linen worth £100,000 per annum. The occupation of the handloom weaver had much to commend it, there being effective apprenticeship requirements only in a few areas such as Dunfermline where up until 1828 the weavers had managed to hold the restrictions of their ancient guild intact. Many weavers worked in their own homes, obtaining their yarn from a merchant to whom they sold their finished "wab". They could work at their own speed and so vary their earnings according to their needs, and those who took a pride in their work could command better prices because of its greater uniformity or complexity. Each weaver was therefore his 'own boss' and, not surprisingly perhaps, was inclined to be an individualist and very independent in thought, action and deed. The weavers were considered very skilled and intelligent men and because they had a common interest and a long tradition of strong craftsmanship they were seen as a potent social force and capable of determined concerted action when the need arose.

Around 1830, political protests were a common sight in Dunfermline especially on the question of the vote for the working man. The franchise being confined, in effect, to property owners and landed proprietors, many of the politically conscious and underprivileged were campaigning to bring pressure on the Government. By 1832 this pressure had become so effective that the franchise was extended to the middle classes (First Reform Bill). Though this measure had some limited effect it still disenfranchised the vast majority of ordinary people and the weavers of Dunfermline were in the forefront of a movement which ultimately led to the Chartist risings in various parts of the country.

Lauder, always listening and learning, took a keen and active interest in the political unrest and inevitably came into close contact with the leaders of this movement. Amongst these, probably the most outspoken and influential, were two by the name of Thomas Morrison, father and son. Both were men of some education who had seen better days. Old Tom Morrison had been a leather merchant conducting a tanning business in Dunfermline and enjoying some degree of stability which was to prove, as in so many other cases, to have been on the artificial stimulus given to the home trade by the Napoleonic wars. When these ended with Waterloo in 1815, his business collapsed and was obliged to diversify his leather trade into shoemaking. He spent his days clad in a leather apron hammering out his living on a cobbler's lap-stone, yet all of his spare hours were devoted to study and public speaking in the hope of furthering the conditions of his own social class. Leaving his shop he could be seen walking along unfrequented roads with stacks of books and papers under his arm to villages and hamlets where he would speak to gatherings in the open air or perhaps in the local church or school. From these speeches thousands of weavers, colliers and others gained their first knowledge of the new discoveries that marked the dawn of the nineteenth century. But it was the social and political themes that were nearest to his heart. Speaking constantly against the prevailing political system, his platform performances left a lasting impression on many including young George Lauder who listened and learned many things.

Old Morrison at this time was the friend and follower of William Cobbet, the nineteenth century radical who along with Henry Hunt and others were intensely active outside Parliament for the reform of the political system. A letter from Morrison to Cobbet in 1833 shows how the seeds of George Lauder's own great educational campaign were being sown. In this letter old Morrison criticises the existing system of education in an essay entitled "Headucation and Handucation" in which he declares that practice must be combined with theory. Mr Morrison's article was printed in pamphlet form and circulated throughout Fife. Morrison even founded a journal of his own, The Precursor, which was so radical that the Dunfermline printer refused to set it up and it had to be printed in Edinburgh.

George Lauder came under the influence of Old Tom Morrison and as a young man became a follower of Morrison's philosophy of egalitarian democracy and the Chartist cause. He also came under the influence of one of Morrison's four daughters, Seaton Morrison. Mutual attraction ripened into affection and we find young George Lauder, barely out of his teens, a very happy young man and, through his courtship of Seaton, a frequent visitor at the Morrison home. At about the same time another of the Morrison girls, Margaret, had found a similar love match with another weaver by the name of William Carnegie, who being some years older than George had been in a position to marry Margaret and set up house in a small cottage in Moodie Street, with his loom on the ground floor and the living quarters above. George Lauder and Seaton Morrison were welcome guests in a home which had been founded on the kind of culture and traditions they themselves had been used to, and so the sisters were drawn closer together whilst the two men became good friends and had a great deal in common to discuss. Both were weavers, both were readers, and both were interested in poetry, music, politics and religion. These subjects were discussed in an atmosphere of harmony and mutual understanding and in a spirit of genuine love for their fellow men and country.

In 1835 a third member was added to the Carnegie household when Margaret Carnegie gave birth to a son named Andrew, according to custom, after his paternal grandfather. Shortly after this momentous event and within days of George Lauder reaching his twenty-first birthday, he and Seaton Morrison were married. It was not long before history repeated itself when Seaton Lauder gave birth to a son, George, again named after the paternal grandfather. It was duly written into the Parish Register by Old Tom Morrison himself! That same year Lord Shaftesbury was petitioned by 200 Sunday School teachers, who assured him of the uselessness of attempting to teach factory children owing to their extreme weariness from overwork in the mills and coalmines. In those factories fortunate enough to have some form of education for the child employees, education fees were deducted from the children's wages.

For George and Seaton Lauder the first year of married life was not without its anxieties. There had been another recession in trade and it was very difficult to find buyers for cloth. So many weavers were out of work that jobs were being found for them at a pittance in road and street repairs. A number of the younger men abandoned the craft and took work in one of the numerous local coalmines that peppered the County of Fife. To add to the uneasiness of the young parents, there was a serious outbreak of typhus and measles which caused some two hundred deaths in the burgh within the year. George Lauder and William Carnegie frequently discussed the future of their chosen trade. The Industrial Revolution was by now well under way and was having its effect on textile manufacturing. The spinning process had been the first to be affected by the new wave of mechanisation. Watt's steam engine coupled with the ingenious contrivances of Hargreaves, Arkwright and Crompton in cotton spinning had

Bailie Tom Morrison, George Lauder's brother-in-law, was a member of Dunfermline Town Council for more than forty years and, alongside Lauder, was a champion of the Chartist cause in Fife.

# THE PRECURSOR,

## A Dunfermline Monthly Newspaper.

No II.  FRIDAY, FEBRUARY 1 1833  PRICE TWOPENCE

### TO OUR READERS.

IT were ungrateful not to acknowledge the very encouraging measure of public favour with which the PRECURSOR has been received. Our sales have come up fully to our expectations; the expression of a friendly feeling has met us in all quarters, from men of all political parties, among all the grades of society; we have heard of no attempt at ridicule—no invective—no hypercriticism; even our shortcomings have been excused, and our errors passed over. We admire your liberality and thank you for your kindness.

We have further to express our regret, that we cannot, in the present number, evince our gratitude by enlarged columns or reduced price, and other intended improvements,—all which we hope soon to realize. The day has been, when, flattered with such prospects of usefulness,—if not of fame, we would at once have rushed forward in the ranks, and sought the front of periodical literature. But now, age, or experience, or something, cries, Hooly! and the distich of Franklin is more remembered than a common sermon—

"Vessels large may venture more,
But little boats must keep near shore."

Had other inducements to caution been necessary, we have one in the advice of a gentleman, prudent as he is patriotic, and honest as he is wise.—" One item of advice I will alone offer to you, and that is, not to involve yourself in any expense that may bring you into difficulties, as you will thereby distress yourself, and injure those you cannot pay. Besides, NO MAN who is in debt can be an INDEPENDENT MAN. With your opinions, as expressed in the letter, it would be very mortifying to be obliged to forfeit that independence you have, through any wish to improve others, however praiseworthy such attempt might be.—JOSEPH HUME."

We had thus written and concluded, when we saw ourselves honoured with the notice of the Fife Herald. It was kindly done, by the correspondent in Dunfermline. " Its politics are of the extreme radical"—Well, so much the better. But it is thought it will not see another number"—So, was the wish father to the "(thought?". Then, Mr Scribie, you see now that the " thought" was a wrong one." Pray, say so, when you write to the Herald another of your bits o' pitiful piddling letters. Please add, that it is now " thought" the PRECURSOR may see as many numbers as did the GREAT GASOMETER, though certainly, we shall not affect any thing like the " fun and fire" emitted from that bright luminary, especially, in the ever-memorable " chit chat" department. Nay, you may tell the Herald, that it is even " thought" the PRECURSOR, undaunted as it is with pictures of bears, elephants, &c, may travel in company with the sapient SCRAP BOOK; and it is even " thought" it doubtful which of the two may first reach the end of its journey." One word more you may add, that it will not be the jealousy of the Dunfermline printers, or rather its own printers and booksellers, that will stop the progress of the PRECURSOR.

We turn from the contemptible littleness we have witnessed, to the enlightened and liberal public. Is it not shameful that while Stirling, Kirkaldy, and Cupar, has each its periodical press, Dunfermline should lag behind, having no organ whatever through which its intelligent inhabitants may communicate their opinions and sentiments? We have attempted to supply the desideratum. It is with you to show whether we shall be ultimately successful.

Tradesmen and Mechanics, in particular! the PRECURSOR and its successor are devoted to your interests. Let every two of you club a penny a-month each, or every four a half-penny each, and a large sheet will be open for you, in which you may publish your grievances, your wants, and your wishes. Like Mr Atkinson, we are of, from, and for you; and on your support we would chiefly depend.

A copy of 'The Precursor' written and edited by Andrew Carnegie's Grandfather Thomas Morrison (Bailie Morrison). This newspaper was so radical for its time that the Dunfermline printers refused to print it after only four editions and it then had to be printed in Edinburgh. It was the champion of the Chartist cause.

A sketch of early Dunfermline taken when George Lauder was only seventeen years of age.
As a weaver, Lauder took a great deal of interest in the rise of the Chartist movement spurred on by the
First Reform Bill of 1832, an extension of the voting rights to include the middle classes.  (DPL LHC)

The Heugh Mills which formed part of Pittencrieff estate. A dam led water to provide power to operate three mills. The top mill produced flour, the middle mill produced meal and the bottom mill was where George Lauder's father produced snuff.

had their influence on the flax side of the industry and had inevitably resulted in the opening of Dunfermline's first spinning mill a few years previous. Now there were seven such mills in the burgh but even then, the weavers were still confident and hopeful that the more complex and intricate process of weaving could not lend itself to a machine operation.

These facts were known and understood by both Lauder and Carnegie, but the two men drew different conclusions. At the age of 33 William Carnegie may have been capable of clearer judgement, but he had descended from several generations of handloom weavers and as a result may have been swayed by sentiment rather than reason. He deplored the introduction of mechanisation, predicted the failure of the new factories, and believed that neither in quality nor in the production, especially of damask, could the handloom be superseded. Moreover he held that the present depression was only a passing phase, that there had always been ups and downs in the weaving industry and always would be.

By contrast George Lauder, though by ten years the younger man, was a careful, methodical thinker who had a habit of marshalling his facts and looking them straight in the face. He had come to the conclusion that, for handloom weaving, as with hand spinning, the writing would eventually be on the wall. He saw a bleak future ahead for the handloom weavers and none in pressing his opinions on William Carnegie who was not to be convinced.

There was no family tradition of weaving in Lauder's case to cloud his business judgement. Having avoided snuff milling as a career because of that industry's decline, he now found himself in an occupation whose continued existence was similarly threatened. Prudence urged him out before it was too late. With this conviction, his real problem became a domestic one, namely was Seaton prepared to share with him the risks and hardships which might come with a change of occupation? History reveals that she was at one with him. She was a Morrison and a fighter, she shared her husband's opinions and was prepared to support him in his short and long-term ideas.

Having waited his time until a suitable opportunity presented itself, Lauder became a blacksmith, a trade which was basic and therefore a bit more secure. Little is known of the details of his new occupation except that the work was heavy, arduous and a tax on his physical resources. Day after day he would come home completely exhausted by the rigours of the unaccustomed heavy toil. He would not be easily discouraged and it is quite probable that, at first, he expected that his aching muscles would become quite used to it after a spell and that he would be able to take the daily tasks in his stride. But he had not foreseen the levels of strength and stamina which was required on a daily basis. A few months at this occupation were to prove that determination alone was not enough. Though tall and well-built Lauder was neither muscular nor robust, and it became evident that if he was to persist it would be at the expense of his health. He eventually had to abandon this second attempt at a career, though possibly not before he had saved up some money for a small deposit on some future business venture. George Lauder eventually found the occupation for which he would be most suited, that of working for himself as a grocer in Guildhall Street.

Guildhall Street, where George Lauder first set up his grocer business in 1840.
In his own words: "I found myself at the age of 25 at the back of a counter with a deficient education for the trade I had engaged in." (DPL LHC)

His frank recognition of his own deficiencies in knowledge and experience of the grocery business and his determination to make a success of it this time made him a willing learner and a tireless worker. Fortunately, his new career happened to coincide with an increase in the nation's general prosperity. The same good fortune which had now enabled William Carnegie to enlarge his weaving business enabled George Lauder to find his feet as a shopkeeper. This turning-point in his life came at a time when the whole nation began to observe with a mixture of enthusiasm and indifference such events as the wedding of Queen Victoria, the Chimney Sweeps Act (passed without the slightest attention of the private landlords, local authorities and magistrates, who continued to use small children to sweep chimneys who often got stuck and lost their lives) and the Penny Post. These were happy times for both the Lauders and the Carnegies. The long hours worked ensured business success which in turn brought reasonable comfort to the families at a time when their two sons were reaching an interesting age. Young Andrew Carnegie was a loveable little terror and always wanted to go and see his new cousin, young George Lauder.

At two years of age Andrew could not get his tongue round the name George, so he had to be content to call him "Dod" or "Doddie". When in due course it was Dod's turn to try to say the name of cousin Andrew Carnegie, his first efforts, to the delight of his audience, blurted out the word "Naig" and thus it was to remain that throughout their long lives they were always to be known as Dod and Naig to each other.

The two cousins spent much time in each other's company particularly on a Sunday when Lauder was free from his everyday commitments. Being very fond of children, especially George and Andrew, he had a great deal of patience and resource which were needed with the two, especially the young 'Naig.' Lauder would take them almost every Sunday for a walk around that part of the Abbey which overlooked the Glen and the two boys were completely enthralled. His expertise with nature and the children ensured that their walks together abounded with natural interest. Lauder was well aware that a sudden change in temperature, soil or climate would retard the growth of a young plant and in like manner any sudden transition could be detrimental to a child's progress. The pupil - teacher who had not quite forgotten his own childish exploits and who was never too conscious of the dignity of his new educational position became a valuable teacher.

The places, the trees, the flowers and the birds were all invested with a mingling of fact and fancy as would appeal to children most. Lauder was so passionately fond of the wild flowers that he could not bear to see them being pulled and he instructed his pupils accordingly. They might look at the flowers, study their beauty and smell their fragrance but they were not allowed to pull them. In the flowers, he told them, lived other little creatures, and to pluck the flowers was to deprive them of their homes. Instead, at his suggestion, Dod and Naig would kneel down and look closely under the petals where they would find little surprises of sweets. Lauder had put them there as a reward for not having pulled the flowers and disturbed the creatures' homes. In these walks they lived in a wonderland of delight, the boys listening, learning and losing themselves and Lauder supremely happy to enjoy their innocent charm.

They would then return home to the Lauder or the Carnegie home where Margaret and Seaton were busy with their own discussions and precious respite from the 'bairns' and William Carnegie would set aside his book for a 'chin-wag' with George on the pressing issues of the day. In close conformity with the Morrison tradition, their politics were of the most radical nature for their times, and as such, from their frequent public appearances, they were well known and very well respected.

What they did not wear so readily on their sleeve, but which was nevertheless of deep concern to both of them, was that for a long time neither of them had been able to find comfort or conviction in the orthodox religion of their day. They had, however, finally found satisfaction, thanks to the influence of a remarkable man and member of a remarkable family, Joseph N. Paton. Originally attached to the Established Church, but being dissatisfied, Paton had become a Methodist, then a Quaker, and had finally found what he was seeking in the doctrines of Emanuel Swedenborg. He built a little chapel in the grounds of his own home in Wooers' Alley and there, with no attempt to dissuade anyone from normal church attendance or membership, he expounded the doctrines of that philosopher to a select few who shared his quest for "God, avoidance of evil, and the performance of good deeds." Amongst the sixty people who associated themselves with the chapel were George Lauder, William Carnegie and Tom Morrison.

The period of prosperity proved to be all too short. In 1842 there was a shortage of work and many of the weavers again were destitute. The causes were not far to seek. Officially, to protect British agriculture against the importation of foreign grain, a "Corn Law" had been passed in 1815 prohibiting the importation of wheat except when its price inside the country rose to eighty shillings a quarter. It was hailed by landowners and agriculturists (in whose interests it had been framed) as a beneficial measure, and was initially so accepted by the mass of town dwellers, including the burghers of Dunfermline.

George Lauder was one of the first locals to question its wisdom and to point out to his fellow men that it would be the cause of their distress, because it would not only keep up the price of their staple diet, but also by restraining imports prevent export of their manufactured goods and thus not only make the cost of food high, but prevent them from earning the money to buy it. His contentions, it seemed, received little attention until droughts in the year 1837 and 1838 forced some rethinking. In 1839 news of the formation of an Anti Corn Law League in Manchester and the campaign by Richard Cobden (himself a farmer), completely vindicated Lauder's earlier diagnosis of the case.

Now that adversity was upon them once again, the weavers went into action, and this time they were joined by the colliers and other workers. George Lauder took a lesser part in the movement at this time, partly because the building up of his business was making demands on what would have been his leisure, but also because an addition to the family was imminent. Tommy Morrison, however, alone now since the death of his father Old Tom, led the campaign in a concerted plan for the "Peaceful Cessation from Labour" ('a general strike'). The military were called in to subdue the strikers, and Tommy, having led his men with great ability and restraint, was nevertheless arrested and locked up in the Town Jail. In July 1842, before these upheavals had culminated, Lauder was urgently called to his wife's bedside. The birth of their new baby had been terribly complicated and both his wife Seaton and the infant tragically died as a result. Lauder was utterly devastated. Heartbroken for months, he sought relief from his grief in three directions - his work in the shop, the care of the children, Dod and Naig, and a resumption of his political interests and activities.

Lauder set out to develop the character of the two boys, and did so by going down to eye-level with them, so that he could thoroughly understand them and by sounding the right chords they could understand him. *"I made myself a child, so that they might be men"*, he said afterwards. He endowed their imagination with two heroes, Sir William Wallace and Robert Bruce, and had taught them the glories of both before they had even learned to read. The room at the back of Lauder's grocer shop, in a sense, became the first Lauder school and, after hours, a kind of workshop theatre. Naig and Dod became the first students of Lauder who had carefully selected educational games, plays and passages that were colourful, possessed action, and allowed free rein to the emotions. Shakespeare's Historical Dramas, 'The Lady of the Lake' and Mary Queen of Scots were among the favourites. But it was the tragedy of the Douglas which brought lasting local fame to the young boys. In full rehearsal, Dod played Norval, Naig played Glenalvon, while Lauder, to permit the boys full scope, contented himself with the minor part of Lord Randolph.

The childhood training they received from Lauder was by no means all poetry and drama. They were often called upon to assist in the running of the Lauder grocery business. They ran errands, served at the counter and carried out (behind the scenes) sweeping-up, stocktaking, book-keeping and making up accounts according to their capacity. This was no pretence. This was for real and all the time they would be listening and learning. There was even a time when their services were enlisted to avert a business crisis. In the summer of 1845, Lauder had found himself with too many gooseberries and seeing that they were about to be a loss unless promptly sold, called the boys and asked if they would go to Crossgates with John Vick and his "Cuddy Cart" and try and sell them. It was a big job but Lauder never once underestimated the intelligence or abilities of the two young lads. Gaining courage from Lauder's confidence in them, the two set off next day on their important mission. They returned late in the evening wildly excited and very proud men having sold every one of the gooseberries; the situation was saved. It was a very practical lesson in enterprise, self-reliance and courage but most importantly it gave the two boys a great sense of achievement and self worth which they would build and develop the rest of their lives.

About a year after Old Tom Morrison died, things were at their lowest ebb in Dunfermline. Seven hundred men with nine hundred dependants were completely without any means of financial support. To prevent actual starvation, 'soup-kitchens' had to be opened at public expense. The crisis became so great that the Town Council had to borrow to the limit of its credit to see it through this critical time. George Lauder and Will Carnegie, along with others, were arguing, petitioning, addressing meetings and throwing their full weight behind the political campaign for a repeal of the Corn Laws, Universal Suffrage and recognition for a People's Charter.

Naig and Dod had by now started formal schooling, and the former now had a younger brother, Thomas Morrison Carnegie. Meanwhile, in October 1843, George Lauder got married once again to a local lass by the name of Margaret Haig and in due course their first daughter, Margaret, was born on 12th July 1844. A second daughter, Elizabeth, was born on 6th August 1846 and when their third and final daughter, Ann, was born on 1st December 1850, the family circle was complete.

George Lauder and his second wife Margaret Haig who were married in October 1843. Lauder was involved with Bailie Morrison in the achievement of a repeal of the Corn Laws in 1846.

Following the death of his first wife Seaton in 1842 George Lauder remarried in 1843 a local lass by the name of Margaret Haig. This is a rare photograph of George Lauder, the family man, with his three daughters Ann, seated by her father's knee, Elizabeth, behind Ann, and Margaret, standing on Lauder's right.

Tommy Morrison, since his stretch in the Town Jail and because of his dignified behaviour in controlling the rioters, even from within the prison walls, had so gained the confidence of both public and magistrates that he was elected to the Town Council and even became a Bailie, so that he was henceforth to be known as 'The Bailie.' This added weight to the Morrison, Lauder and Carnegie campaigns, which were enhanced when their first objective was achieved with the repeal of the Corn Laws in 1846. Through days of torrential rain, triumphal arches were erected, bands played and processions threaded the streets in celebration. Expectations were high as their thirty-five year campaign had finally been recognised. Heartened by their success the Radicals were ready to channel their efforts into their other objective, a forthcoming election. Dunfermline at this time was within the parliamentary constituency of "Stirling Burghs" and since Inverkeithing, South Queensferry and Culross made up three out of four partners the area could exert considerable pressure.

The Dunfermline Radicals played their part in promoting John Benjamin Smith, a Lancashire man who had been president of the Anti Corn League, as the Liberal candidate nomination against the Tory John Maitland. Both Lauder and Bailie Morrison were on the local Committee and they were proud to be able to bring to Dunfermline the famous John Bright, friend of Cobden. Lauder tells the story:

*"It looked as though the campaign was going very well in Fife and that this would sway the constituency in favour of the Liberal, when the rival party took an unexpectedly strong line by proclaiming that Smith, the Liberal, was a Unitarian and Placarding the district with the slogan: "WOULD YOU VOTE FOR A UNITARIAN?"*

This was serious and had to be countered. News came in that the blacksmith at Cairneyhill, who was also the Chairman of Smith's Committee in that village, was saying that he would never vote for a Unitarian. Lauder went over to remonstrate with him and the following conversation took place over a dram in the village inn.

*Blacksmith:* "Man, Ah canna vote for a Unitarian!"
*Lauder:* "But Maitland's a Trinitarian!"
*Blacksmith:* "Damn. That's wurse! Ah'll vote fur Smith efter a'."

Smith won by a small majority.

Thus the Radicals obtained two of their objectives in rapid succession, and although Universal Suffrage eluded them they did have the satisfaction of seeing cheaper food returning to the land even if it was just for a short while.

In the textile industry, busy times returned and more steam-powered factories were springing up. The vast majority of weavers were now reconciled to the inevitable and recognised that the coming of the machine age was unavoidable. There was however, a hard core who could not or would not make this concession to progress, and William Carnegie was one of them. As times became harder and he found it increasingly difficult to sell his webs, Will Carnegie was obliged to dismiss his men and to sell for shillings the looms that had cost him pounds and had been his pride.

Will Carnegie was a broken man and had no spirit for breaking away from Fife for pastures new. Margaret, however, was extremely determined to get away from it all and to emigrate to America as her brother and sisters had done some time before with measured success. Numerous discussions took place amongst relatives and friends with mixed feelings on the idea. Lauder, in that quiet way that was his, mentally marshalled the facts and faced them squarely. Materially, in Dunfermline things were at their worst and in America they were now on the mend. He was well aware that in some cases emigration had been disastrous, but with relatives to go to, the Carnegies would not be abandoned.

On the human side, he would greatly miss the Carnegies, especially young Andrew who was by now like a second son to him. He also knew that Margaret could never be happy to stay in the Old Country where circumstances had so mocked and wounded her husband and had been so cruel to herself. But above all he recognised in Andrew an ability far beyond the ordinary and a spirit of adventure which was not to be inhibited by the institutions of an old civilisation but set free to spread its wings and soar to its own heights. Lauder saw part of himself in young Andrew and perhaps in anticipation of their eventual emigration had seen to it that Andrew was well aquainted with American history and institutions to a degree beyond that possessed by most Americans of his day.

Lauder was thus on the side of emigration, but in the end it was Margaret herself who took the final big decision to leave Scotland. The details of their journey were meticulously overseen by Lauder and it was a sad party which set out in the horse-drawn omnibus which ran to Charlestown on the same railroad as conveyed the coals there for shipment. The four Carnegies, with Lauder and Tommy Morrison riding with them, did their best to put a brave face on it, but as the top of the Abbey Tower finally disappeared from sight, young Andrew cried. When they reached Charlestown they stepped off the omnibus and walked over to the small boat which was to row them over to the paddle steamer.

Lauder wished to be the last to take leave of young Andrew as they meant so much to each other. Lauder took up a position behind him at the stern, and quietly impressed upon him that where he was going there was room to rise and that he was sure to do well. A few words of advice, and they found themselves at the steamer, with the captain standing on the paddle box calling on the laddie to follow the others aboard, but Naig couldn't move. Lauder put a sovereign in his hand and said; "now Naig, you go." Naig set off, jumped over two or three seats and then turned hastily back, threw his arms around Lauder's neck and cried, *"I canna leave ye! I canna leave ye!"* Lauder gently loosened Naig's arms, helped by a kind sailor who carried the inconsolable lad to the steamer and lifted him aboard, declaring it the saddest parting he had ever witnessed.

With the Carnegies now gone and young Dod attending school, Lauder had a little more time to concentrate on his daughters and to pursue the many other activities which were close to his heart. One of his favourite meeting places was the home of Joseph Paton, leader of the Dunfermline Swedenborgians. Here George Lauder would divide his evenings between discussions of immortal glory over a game of chess and spending an hour or two listening while someone held him spellbound with the violin.

When seen on the High Street Lauder, now in his late thirties, was always clad in a long brown cape reaching almost to his knees. He was tall and slender with a slight stoop and his head topped with a high hat. His whole figure moved with a deliberate tread and he outwardly portrayed the gentle mystic tendencies that made up his inner life. His head too, with a lofty brow canopied by light brown silken hair, the deep grey eyes, quiet and wistful, and the large but delicately cut features, was a noble one. Manifestly here was a soul who found his chief delight in flowers, birds, music, poetry and legend.

In his grocer's shop Lauder succeeded so well that he was able to move from Guildhall Street to the more prosperous High Street; number eight. This shop ran through to Maygate, and hence it was when Mr Blelloch, the original owner of the property, erected new buildings in Maygate that Mr Lauder was able to acquire one of the new shops. Surrounded by barrels of whiting and salt herring, almost hidden at times by sacks of potatoes and onions, George Lauder would not, at first, have been taken for the living embodiment of Scottish glory.

Yet even in these surroundings Lauder was impressive. He was by now a prominent figure locally, a keen radical who possessed the courage of his convictions. In the 1850s Lauder was always remembered as one of the few men who publicly denounced England's great but futile adventure in the Crimean War.

Lauder was also a great champion in the preservation of human and public rights. With no Health and Safety policy, accidents in factories were rife and in the first half of 1850 out of 323 factory accidents, 183 of them were children. The factory Inspector obligingly recorded that the accidents were due to *"carelessness on the part of the individuals themselves."*

Many owners were making steady protests against a law compelling them to release children under 13 years of age from their factories so many hours a week for the purpose of education. To get around the law of releasing their child employees they devised complex shift systems. In 1856 it was estimated that less than one-third of Scots factory children could read or write, many working in foundries ten or twelve hours daily at the tender age of eight or nine.

These and other injustices formed part of the broader campaign by Lauder and the Chartists to extend the franchise and introduce a system of accountability and democracy into the country as well as the workplace. In connection with a dispute with one Mr Hunt of Pittencrieff estate regarding some vacant ground, Mr Lauder was said to have been more than a 'moving spirit' in the tearing down of a barricade erected by Mr Hunt to keep out the so-called undesirables.

Dunfermline interest in the early 1860s was absorbed by the ethics and effects of the American Civil War. "The War" had taken the place of the Corn Laws, the People's Charter and the Reform Ballot as the great topic of public discussion. The American south had become a cotton empire and nearly four million slaves were employed and were seen as an absolutely essential element in Southern prosperity. But if slavery paid, it left men with uneasy consciences. This unease became most evident in the North, where a man who demanded the abolition of slavery could comfort himself with the reflection that the financial loss which abolition would entail would, after all, be borne by someone else - his neighbour in the south.

Popular sentiment in Dunfermline was against the North, and young pioneers like Andrew Carnegie were amazed that his native town, for generations the home of radicalism, always foremost in the championship of freedom and democratic ideas, should favour the Southern cause. That Dunfermline had suffered from the War is true, since America was the best customer for its linens and orders had naturally decreased, but Lancashire was suffering even more, yet this part of England remained loyal to the North. Only a few important men in Dunfermline favoured the Federal Government. One of them was George Lauder. His admiration for America had only grown with its misfortunes. His confidence in the Northern armies never wavered, and the vigour with which he was fighting Lincoln's battles brought him into conflict with his fellow citizens.

Lauder gave more than oratorical support, for he entrusted practically all his life savings to Carnegie for investment in Federal bonds, securities which, at the time, English bankers regarded as untrustworthy. Lauder's money was offered at a time when the fortunes of the Union were most desperate and when gold was quoted at three times the value of American currency.

*"Invest this for me as you think best,"* said Uncle Lauder to Andrew Carnegie, *"but if you put it into United States bonds it will add to my pleasure, for then I can feel that, in the hour of her danger, I have never lost faith in the Republic."*

Following the American Civil War George Lauder, whose investments had doubled in value with the Union's victory, sent Andrew Carnegie a piece of damask linen with an inscription of thanks woven into it: "To Andrew Carnegie from his friend George Lauder of Dunfermline 1865". This is now in the Andrew Carnegie Birthplace Museum.

George Lauder continued to remain active in all aspects of family and political life for many years. For a period of three weeks during the long dry summer of 1870 water was carried in barrels to the higher parts of Dunfermline. Even in the lower parts of the town, domestic supplies were only available from 8.00 am until 11.00 am. Water shortages had been a regular problem in the Town for the previous 150 years as its population grew and the demand increased. Various means had been considered to improve the town's supply but to no avail. However, on 26th January 1871, George Lauder put forward to the Town Council a far-reaching scheme for obtaining a supply from the River Devon. His letter was accompanied by a plan, estimate and analysis prepared by Mr R B Symington of Dunfermline. This proposal was to bring down 2,000,000 gallons of water per day to the reservoirs at Craigluscar for the supply of the West of Fife by means of 'clay pipes' more than half way with a fall of three feet per mile, and 10,000 yards of iron pipes with a compensation pond there for the supply of the river, the estimated cost being £30,000.

This proposal went to a vote to find out the feelings of the 20,000 inhabitants towards the idea. A plebiscite resulted in an overwhelming majority against the scheme and it was abandoned. Lauder again put forward the plan to the Town Council on 23rd February and was once again left on the table. Seven months later on 25th September 1871 Lauder sent a petition to the Town Council from 1,397 ratepayers complaining about the water situation and requesting the Council apply for Parliamentary powers to abstract supplies from the River Devon. Consideration was postponed meanwhile pending an investigation again of the Craigluscar resources.

Water supplies became scarce again in 1873 and this time the water was shut off from 8.00 pm till 7.00 am for 42 nights, much to the anger and frustration of the local population who forwarded a letter to the Town Council requesting immediate action, *"to introduce a greatly enlarged supply of what is at once a prime necessity of life for the inhabitants."*

Mr Hunt of Pittencrieff, at this time offered terms to the Council, to all his rights in the Town Loch as an additional supply, terms which the Council found unacceptable.

George Lauder would write copious letters in support of the Devon scheme and when there was a lapse in correspondence, as there often was in the local press, he would write anonymous letters to back up his claim and to provoke some local reaction, as on 16th August 1873:

*"Sir,*
*I've been wondering whether you'll print a few words frae a puir body like me, about the dirty watter we're getting doon here I' the Netherton. It's a shame for us to ha'e to mak kail to oor bairns o't. But whit can we dae, when we canna get ony better? I think if some o' the wives in every street wad tak my advice, they wad gang to the provost and tell him that we canna bear it ony langer, and that he maun jist tak Mr Lauder's plan an bring in the Devon. If this wis dune, I warrant ye wad get plenty o' watter, an no be lang till't. I'll no sign my ain name, for I dinna want onybody to ken that I've written tae the press, but I'll just sign myself,*
*Yours, &."*

Severe water shortages were again experienced in June 1874 and June 1875 and were followed by numerous complaints from the ratepayers which included voices from Townhill. Water had also to be found to fill the new Baths presented to the people of Dunfermline by Andrew Carnegie which only added to the problem.

Pressure by Mr Lauder and his supporters in the form of another petition signed by 2,166 ratepayers was placed on the Town Council to adopt the Devon scheme. On Friday 24th October 1875, the Council heard a deputation which included George Lauder of Chalmers Street, Dunfermline. As the supply at this time was only on 13 hours per day, the desired effect resulted and the Town Council agreed to ask Messrs J & A Leslie, Edinburgh, to advise on the scheme. On Wednesday 6th October 1875 a combined Committee of the Town Council representatives and the deputation (including Lauder) met Mr Leslie at Rumbling Bridge and proceeded to examine the River Devon and its tributaries. Mr Leslie was asked to bear in mind that the supply to the town had been cut off for 42 nights in 1873, 39 nights in 1874 and 101 nights in 1875, from 8pm till 7am.

At a meeting of this joint Committee on 12th October 1875, Mr Leslie presented a preliminary report advising in favour of the Glendevon water supply. He gave a rough scheme, utilising the tributaries of the Devon on the west side, for one million gallons per-day, estimated cost of £60,000 and for three quarter million gallons per-day, estimated cost £58,000. Full support was given to the project and the Committee authorised the preparations of plans and an application to Parliament for powers to execute. Even at this stage a group of ratepayers were against the idea and a deputation urged the Town Council to cancel the whole thing. Not to be put off, the protesting ratepayers presented a petition to the Town Council with 2,334 signatures against the scheme for the Glendevon project opting instead for that of the Craigluscar project. This petition was later compared with Mr Lauder's on a valuation basis, and from this it became clear that the Glendevon supporters of Mr Lauder were nearly double than those in favour of the Craigluscar scheme.

A Parliamentary Bill was deposited on 24th December 1875 and as a result all opposition to the scheme was dropped. On Friday 29th June 1877 the Town Council, accompanied by officials and the engineer, proceeded to Glensherup to witness the formal cutting of the first sod of the new water works. On 6th September 1878 the town was, for the first time, supplied with water direct from Glensherup, a tributary to Glendevon, which gave a total daily supply of 3,000,000 gallons.

Between 1958 and 1961 modernisation of the Glensherup Reservoir was undertaken. With this modernisation its original lifespan of 80 years was extended indefinitely and indeed it has continued to provide good water in abundance as was first envisaged by George Lauder all those years ago. Proof, if proof were needed, that he had the foresight and understanding of what was required well ahead of the times in which he lived. Lauder applied this same mode of creative thinking in all aspects of his life but none more so than in the field of education. It was Lauder's involvement with Scottish education more than with any other aspect of social history that the key to his great stature lay. *"The use of the saw, chisel, brace and bit; that was the education I had"* said Lauder in 1899, . . . *"and I always look back with satisfaction on having been taught this early to use my hands."*

Lauder brought a keen and critical mind to the subject of education at a time when the general ethos of Scottish education in the mid to late nineteenth century had very simple aims. Firstly to provide as cheaply as possible the bulk of the population with the bare minimum of elementary education combined with adequate social discipline. Secondly, to give a small number of children of all classes, but especially the higher classes, a more respectable academic education to qualify them for their role as a controlling elite.

It was never intended that education for the vast majority should go beyond the three Rs, though some provision had always been made for a select few of the common people to go on to do further training in Latin as a preparation for higher education. It needed time and hard work by people like George Lauder for Scotland to have any real level of autonomy over its educational affairs. Even the 1872 Act made no provision for state-supported education above the elementary level. The needs of secondary education, as with practical training, was given no consideration. George Lauder's crusade was for an entirely fresh outlook on secondary education and was directed towards a system of free schooling and the inclusion within the curriculum of some form of technical training. He spoke from experience as well as from the heart when he stated: *"I resolved that every youth that came under my influence would get a good technical and literary training."*

It was his desire that young workers in training should learn the manual crafts of experimentation and apply it in building their own equipment. They needed to get the feel, so to speak, of tools and techniques so as to appreciate their own potential and limitations.

As early as 1835 Lauder's own views had been given a boost by an Edinburgh lawyer who came to address a Dunfermline audience on the subject of "Free Education from the School to the University" and throughout the rest of the century Lauder had that ultimate aim in mind including, as a first step, working progressively for a vast reduction in school fees. With regard to the curriculum, Lauder maintained that: *"It was especially intended for boys who wished to go to University"* and therefore advocated that, *"the curriculum be extended to all modern requirements for industrial education."* This was a clear and far-sighted shift in emphasis from the purely academic to the more practical requirements of industry and society in general.

In the field of technical education he was equally clear and far-sighted in realising the need for a new approach to suit changing industrial conditions. Two important and topical points emerge from his statement that *"apprentices require access to technical and literary education."* Firstly, the reference to technical as meaning directly applied to a particular trade. Secondly, the insistence on "literary education" as an equally important part of that training.

Lauder was on the Burgh School Board no fewer than four times during a period of service which stretched over twelve years. He was first elected to the Dunfermline School Board in 1876 and so began a long series of confrontations between him and the local School Board authorities in his pursuit for genuine educational progress. At a public meeting "to review the past and consider the future requirements of the School Board" strong objection was taken to a grant system: *"why should the working man pay for the education of the upper classes?"*

Lauder who was present at the meeting took it upon himself to let them hear the other side of the argument. He expressed regret to hear the sentiments that had come from the platform. He went on to say that as far back as 1835 he had supported an Edinburgh lawyer who lectured in Dunfermline on free education. As a working man of Dunfermline he protested against the "meanness" that had come from the platform that night. Amid great applause the meeting erupted in howls of protest. Lauder had to withdraw the word "meanness" and substitute "ungenerous" but by this time the point had been made. One local Burgh member practically ordered Mr Lauder from the platform. After quiet had been restored, Lauder proposed to reduce the school fees in the short term and ultimately that the school should be supported from the rates. The meeting broke up in confusion.

At a meeting in August 1884 Lauder moved a motion to the effect that the time had come to introduce Science and Drawing into every school in the city and steps taken to establish a practical system of technical education in Fife. His motion read thus: *"This Board is convinced that the necessity has arisen for a practical education for our boys and that a workshop should be established in Roland Street School and a practised man engaged to teach all boys in the sixth and ex-sixth standards the use of tools."*

In supporting his motion Lauder suggested that, *"a practical man be engaged for the school to teach the boys turning, cabinet making and joiner work. We quite admit, as all members of the Board admitted, that the question is one of paramount importance, and it is only but right that it should be thoroughly discussed, but we cannot help pointing out that the case of elementary schools, as at present constituted, anything which is likely to divert the attention of the pupils from what might strictly speaking be termed education, is open to serious objection."*

The local Dunfermline Journal, in a lengthy article of Saturday 9th August 1884, is quoted as saying: *"Mr Lauder is entitled to the very highest praise for the persistency with which he advocated the teaching of drawing in every school under the Board. In a town like Dunfermline, where the success of the staple industry is dependent in a great degree on the excellence of the design, it is of the highest importance that we should have a formidably rising army of designers."*

However they go on to say: *"While we are constrained to speak thus of Mr Lauder's drawing agitation, yet we are not all prepared to look upon his new proposition in such a manner as to induce us to give him a blank cheque for the manner he proposes introducing technical or properly speaking industrial education. . . .We are quite at one with Mr Lauder as to the necessity for teaching the child that manual facility, which is the A B C of all the arts and industries of the world, but if, as in America and other places, the innovation is to be introduced by the slicing of an hour or two off the time presently devoted to arithmetic, grammar, &c., then there can be no doubt that Her Majesty's Inspector would step in and simply say that this cannot be tolerated.*

*Another thing, Mr Lauder's programme is much too narrow, and if an industrial school is to be established it must be done on the lines very much broader than that of pushing a man into a building with two or three hammers and chisels and a number of benches. We do not by any means wish to throw any obstructions in the way of introducing technical education if it is at all practicable, but we are forced to point out that with the taking over of the endowment schools, and the launching of the new High School, the Burgh Board will have enough to do for eighteen months. Mr Lauder's proposal would be so much a leap in the dark as it is at present."*

In 1885 the scheme to erect the new High School by voluntary subscription was launched. Lauder was again elected to the School Board and spoke of the new school as a fresh argument for his proposal to reduce the fees. Once again he fell foul with his arguments for a reduction of fees from ten shillings to seven shillings and sixpence, (a rise of twopence in the rates from ninepence to elevenpence) as a way forward towards his ultimate insistence on a general free education system. He regarded himself as having being elected to the School Board with that main objective in mind. When it had become clear to Lauder that he would be unable to secure agreement or even understanding on this, he had resigned to pursue it in other ways. A letter was sent to the Board in September 1885 in which he states that his reasons for resignation were that the fees were not being reduced and that the curriculum was especially intended for boys who wished to go to University.

Lauder also expressed the view that the new High School should have been available "first" to all the advanced pupils in Dunfermline and afterwards to all people of Fife and indeed Scotland and that the curriculum should have been extended to all the modern requirements for industrial education.

The genuine regret of his colleagues after his resignation from the School Board and their efforts to persuade him to change his mind were a contemporary tribute to the value placed upon his services in the cause of education. The local press wrote: *"If Mr Lauder has cut connections with the School Board, it is a satisfaction to know that he is always with us. He has convictions, and these convictions he continues, with ability and with remarkable persistency, to place before the public every week."*

This is a reference to the fact that Lauder continued tirelessly to write letters to the local newspapers on the pressing need for educational progress, in or out of office. In 1892 the ratepayers again rejected the opportunity of a unique educational advance when Lauder proposed building a purpose-built technical school as a practical way forward in meeting the needs of society and employers. In 1893 Lauder's arguments had begun to take hold within the School Board and when the technical education question came up once more a majority on the Board determinedly decided they would take up Lauder's proposal and build a technical school. However, this caused a flurry of protests and resignations from those still not convinced by Lauder's arguments. Once more the project was shelved. Following more campaigning and more letter writing by Lauder the matter came up in front of the School Board again and was eventually passed on the slimmest of margins, the casting vote of the Chairman. This was still not the end of it. Some Board members were so bitter about the decision that they went to enormous lengths canvassing the citizens and managed to secure 3,700 signatures against the proposals. In the face of such a weight of opinion, the building of the technical school was once more abandoned.

George Lauder took no further part in formal educational affairs choosing instead to campaign in his own way for the progress and advancement of technical education. Following lengthy letters to his nephew Andrew Carnegie in America in September 1897 putting the case for a purpose-built technical College, Lauder asked him if he would consider putting up the funds for such an idea as a way of contributing towards the practical education of the youth and to meeting the real needs of modern industry. Carnegie thought it a grand idea and Lauder now became the medium through which our present College was gifted to the town.

He addressed a letter to the Chairman of the Board in which he said that he had been authorised by one who was a true friend to Dunfermline and a well-wisher of its educational advancements, to say that he was prepared to lay out a sum of £7,000 in the building of and equipment of a purpose built Technical School for the town and beyond.

The gift was later increased to £10,000 and later again, as prices and requirements rose, the gift was increased to £13,000. The new Technical School was officially opened amid great pomp and splendour on Tuesday 10th October 1899 and was formally handed over to the Burgh School Board at a ceremony attended by over five hundred people from Fife and beyond. There were many guest speakers there that day to record the occasion for posterity but one stood out above everyone else with his own deep and genuine recognition for the man to whom he, the town and Scottish education in general owed so much. Andrew Carnegie, during the course of his speech, spoke of his profound appreciation for his Uncle George Lauder when he said:

*"I never interfere with any gift I give. I believe in strict Home Rule. But it would give me, and it would give Mrs Carnegie, genuine pleasure if you would approve of calling this Technical School the Lauder Technical School . . . To my uncle belongs the credit . . . I could not trust myself to tell you what that man has meant to me."*

It was at his father's snuff mill that an indelible impression was created on the senses of young George Lauder who was always listening and always learning. Lauder's greatest joy was in the workshop, designed to render the mill self sufficient in matters of maintenance.

Around 1827 snuff-milling was fast becoming a declining industry so young George Lauder chose handloom weaving instead. Of all the skilled craftsmen in the town, two out of three were weavers. The job of the handloom weaver had much to commend it especially in Dunfermline where up until 1828 the weavers still managed to hold the restrictions of their ancient guild intact.

Some children had to carve an education from the bitter teacher of experience during a lifetime at the shuttle or down the coal mine.

These "learning" days often began at 4 o'clock in the morning working in semi darkness and filth drawing tubs of coal from a coal face 14 hours a day.

George Lauder's grocershop was to the right of William Clark Liddell shop on the left of this High Street photograph taken in 1902. When Lauder was seen in the High Street he wore a long brown cape which reached down to his knees.
Tall and slender with a slight stoop, he always wore a top hat.
(DPL LHC)

**Extract of entries in an OLD PAROCHIAL REGISTER**

*Registration of Births, Deaths and Marriages (Scotland) Act 1965, s.47*

**Parish of** Dunfermline **County of** Fife

Baptisms ~~June~~ 1815 May

David Strachan Weaver at the back of the Dam and Margaret Cowantray his Wife had a Daughter born 28th May baptized 11th June named Margaret. Witnesses Andrew Strachan and David Cusine.

George Lauder Miller in Dunfermline and Margaret Muir his Wife had a Son born 9th May baptized 11th June Named George. Witnesses John Steuart and John Black there

David Hutton Weaver in Dunfermline and Janet McKenlay his Wife had a Daughter born 13th of June baptized 18th named Isabell. Witnesses George McKenlay & Will. Westwood

John Gall Mason in Dunfermline and Henrietta Stevenson his Wife had a Daughter born 17th of May baptized 4th June named Margaret Witnesses James Christie & Will. Westwood.

The above particulars are extracted from a Register of Births and Baptisms dated 9 May 1815

Extract from the Old Parish Register of Dunfermline showing the birth of George Lauder in 1915. *"George Lauder, Miller in Dunfermline and Margaret Muir his wife had a son born 9 May baptized 11 June named George. Witnesses John Stuart and John Black there."*

Minute of Meeting of the School
Board of the Burgh of Dunfermline
held within the Board Room
on Monday the 3rd day of April
1882 at four oclock P.M.

Present
Mr John Ross
  " William Brown
Revd John W Dunbar
  " Alexr Mitchell
Mr Alexr Morton Senr.
  " William Clark
  " R.M. Wilson
  " George Lauder
Revd John Pitt also
Mr Daniel Gorrie as Returning Officer

    The Returning Officer submitted
the following Report vizt.

    Report by Daniel Gorrie Returning Officer
for the Fourth Election of a School Board
of the Burgh of Dunfermline in accordance with
the provisions of the "Education (Scotland) Act
1872" with the General order regulating the
Triennial Election of School Boards issued
by the Lords of the Committee of the Privy
Council on Education in Scotland of
date 30th November 1881.

I have the honor to Report that the following
are the names designations and places of abode
of the Candidates nominated and not withdrawn for the School Board of this
Burgh

An extract from the minute of the meeting of the School Board 1882.

| No | Christian Name & Surname of Candidate | Designation | Place of Abode |
|---|---|---|---|
| 1 | Henry Beveridge | Manufacturer | Comely Park Place |
| 2 | William Brown | Clerk | Downieville Crescent |
| 3 | William Clark | Auctioneer | High Street |
| 4 | Revd John W. Dunbar | Minister of the Gospel | Comely Park |
| 5 | George Lauder | Retired Merchant | Chalmers Street |
| 6 | Revd A. Mitchell D.D. | Minister of the Gospel | McLean Place |
| 7 | John Morrison | Clothier | Buchanan Street |
| 8 | Alexr Morton Senior | Wood Merchant | Whitemyre |
| 9 | Revd John Pitt | Minister of the Gospel | Gibb Street |
| 10 | John Roberton | Toy Merchant | High Street |
| 11 | John Ross | Solicitor | Chapel Street |
| 12 | John Spence | Dresser | High Street |
| 13 | Robert Main Wilson | Landed Proprietor | Fodbank |

And I have further to report that the several Candidates whose nominations were not withdrawn did at the Election on the Twenty eighth day of March Eighteen hundred & eighty two received the number of votes placed opposite their respective names in the subjoined list:—

| No | Christian Name & Surname of Candidate | Designation | Place of Abode | Number of votes given for each Candidate |
|---|---|---|---|---|
| 1 | Henry Beveridge | Manufacturer | Comely Park Place | 449 |
| 2 | William Brown | Clerk | Downieville Crescent | 1592 |
| 3 | William Clark | Auctioneer | High Street | 1090 |
| 4 | Revd John W. Dunbar | Minister of the Gospel | Comely Park | 1262 |
| 5 | George Lauder | Retired Merchant | Chalmers Street | 1049 |
| 6 | Revd A. Mitchell D.D. | Minister of the Gospel | McLean Place | 1221 |
| 7 | John Morrison | Clothier | Buchanan Street | 899 |
| 8 | Alexr Morton Senior | Wood Merchant | Whitemyre | 1177 |
| 9 | Revd John Pitt | Minister of the Gospel | Gibb Street | 1046 |
| 10 | John Roberton | Toy Merchant | High Street | 916 |
| 11 | John Ross | Solicitor | Chapel Street | 1824 |
| 12 | John Spence | Dresser | High Street | 996 |
| 13 | Robert Main Wilson | Landed Proprietor | Fodbank | 1048 |

And accordingly I have to report that of the Candidates above named & designed the following have been duly elected Members of the School Board of the said Burgh vizt.

| 1 | John Ross |
|---|---|
| 2 | William Brown |
| 3 | Revd John W Dunbar |
| 4 | " A Mitchell D.D |
| 5 | Alexr Morton Senior |
| 6 | William Clark |
| 7 | Robert Main Wilson |
| 8 | George Lauder |
| 9 | Revd John Pitt |

92 High St
Dunfermline 30th March 1882

Humbly reported by
(Sigd) D Corrie

Accordingly George Lauder is duly elected on to the Board with a vote of 1049. George Lauder was on the Burgh School Board no fewer than four times but it was his forward thinking ideas which set the heather on fire.

# Andrew Carnegie

*" I could not trust myself to tell you what
that man has meant to me . . ."*

Andrew Carnegie speaking of George Lauder, 1899.

That Andrew Carnegie, philanthropist and King of Steel, should choose the occasion of the opening of the Lauder Technical School to express his own long held private gratitude, love and deep respect for his uncle, George Lauder, was of profound significance. For while it was Carnegie who put up the money for the new Technical School, much to the embarrassment of many on the School Board who had originally been against it, it was George Lauder's enthusiasm and endless campaigning for the progress of education which had inspired it.

*"It is not he who gives money that he never misses who is the real giver"* said Carnegie, *"but the man who gives his heart to the work; and that my uncle Lauder did."*

Andrew Carnegie was born in the attic of a small cottage on the corner of Moodie Street, Dunfermline on Wednesday 25th November 1835 into a hard working pedigree family of radical weavers. The Carnegies (on his father's side) and the Morrisons (on his mother's side), were leaders of the Dunfermline Chartists, a movement for political reform, and were always at the forefront of numerous campaigns for broad sweeping political change. Old grandfather Carnegie, after whom Andrew was named, was the learned "Professor" of a forward-looking set of weavers in the village of Patiesmuir, near Dunfermline, who had established a "College" which castigated leading figures and the legislation of the times with a vicious relentlessness that earned them the fear and respect of their contemporaries. Grandfather Morrison was a shoe-maker and was the unchallenged leader of many popular causes in Dunfermline. He had married an Edinburgh girl of education and grace by the name of Hodge who died while the family was still young. It was from the Morrisons, especially Old Tom the rebel, that Carnegie is said to have inherited his thinking capacity, but not his features: *His nose and chin they threatened ither."*

*"I think my optimistic nature, my ability to shed trouble and to laugh through life, making all my ducks swans, as friends say I do, must have been inherited from this delightful old masquerading grandfather whose name I am proud to bear."* said Carnegie in later years.

But there was another influence in Carnegie's life which meant more to him than anything else in the world, an influence which kindled the spark of his educational desire until it became a raging fire, the influence of his uncle, George Lauder. In Lauder, Andrew Carnegie found the teacher best qualified to satisfy his profound curiosity and give dramatic meaning to the world.

*"My uncle possessed an extraordinary gift of dealing with children and taught us many things. Among others I remember how he taught us British history by imagining each of the monarchs in a certain place upon the walls of the room performing the act for which he was well known. Thus for me King John sits to this day above the mantelpiece signing the Magna Charta, and Queen Victoria is on the back of the door with her children upon her knees"*, said Carnegie with pride.

Carnegie spent most of his youth years between his own home in Moodie Street and his Uncle Lauder's shop in the High Street, Dunfermline. It was here in the back shop of Lauder's grocery business that the origins of a Lauder College first began. A frayed copy of Robert Burns and a few other books sat in an old desk and with this Uncle Lauder taught both boys the poems and songs of the bard, by word of mouth, rewarding them with a penny when they were able to repeat the verses without a break. Along with literature and history and the warm glow of Lauder's charm and soft gentle manner of his patience, these sessions so delighted and inspired young Carnegie. His own father, of which little is known, was constantly tied to his work as a handloom weaver trying to make ends meet while Mrs Carnegie made and mended shoes to supplement their meagre income.

*"Shortly after this I began to learn what poverty meant. Dreadful days came when my father took the last of his webs to the great manufacturer, and I saw my mother anxiously awaiting his return; it was burnt into my heart then that my father had to beg for work; it was then that I resolved to cure that when I got to be a man"* wrote Carnegie.

Carnegie's mother, Margaret, was a strong willed and determined character who desired to achieve affluence and be regarded as the equal of anyone she chose. For Margaret Carnegie, the dwindling of the family income week by week as the industrial revolution dried up the Carnegie sources of income as well as the selling of their business and household goods, was a slow growing shame and young Andrew was extremely conscious of this.

Old William Carnegie's trade had become a prime example of the decline and fall of a prosperous Dunfermline occupation through years of growing industrialisation. Paradoxically, it was the early periods of that industrialisation which had given the weavers a measure of prosperity and which would eventually bring them down. Carnegie claimed that: *"The change from hand-loom to steam-loom weaving was disastrous to our family. My father did not recognise the impending revolution, and was struggling under the old system."*

The education the weavers would have wanted for their children suffered from the need to save every penny they could get and this became a source of bitter regret, more so than any other aspect of their plight. It was thus left, in the main, to Lauder, the High Street grocer and political Radical, who had time free enough to spend in the education of his son and young nephew.

Apart from the memorable education with his Uncle Lauder the only other schooling which Carnegie received during his first thirteen years in Dunfermline was at "Snuffy" Martin's school in Rolland Street. His parents had made a clumsy promise that he would not be sent to school until 'he' asked to go. This caused them no end of anxiety as Carnegie showed little signs of ever asking, but with the help of Lauder and Robert Martin, the schoolmaster, the experience became a pleasant one. Carnegie had learned frugality from his mother and one day when his teacher asked the pupils to recite a proverb from the bible Andrew recited what his mother had told him: *"Look after the pennies and the pounds will look after themselves."* On hearing this, the class broke out in laughter and the teacher stared. Carnegie was indifferent, he had said nothing wrong. After all, he was quoting his mother who was the centre of his life.

He began attending school when he was eight and left when the family emigrated less than five years later. Carnegie was sometimes late in arriving at school on account of his having to bring water from the well at the head of Moodie Street. However, Robert Martin, or "Snuffy" as he was nicknamed, was quite fond of young Carnegie and, knowing the cause, forgave his lateness.

Carnegie may have felt insulted when he was called "Martin's pet" but it was under his severe but efficient eye that he adequately learned his letters by the standards of the old school. The only record of merit which the pupil ever boasted was the award of a penny from Martin, not for excellence in a curriculum subject, but for a successful rendering of a Robert Burns poem, 'Man Was Made to Mourn', mastered in uncle Lauder's back shop and performed with skill before the whole class. *"My good Uncle Lauder justly set great value upon recitation in education, and many were the pennies which Dod and I received for this"* remembered Carnegie. *"'Anything which pleased me I could learn with a rapidity which surprised partial friends. My power to memorise must have been greatly strengthened by the mode of teaching adopted by my uncle Lauder."*

Andrew Carnegie at sixteen (right) and his brother Tom (left). Andrew seemed to inherit all of his mother's energy and used it to the full, always listening and always learning.

As Carnegie grew, Lauder used to take him on trips, mainly to historical and literary shrines. Every Sunday he would take Dod and Naig for a walk around the Abbey to a part that overlooked the Glen. The Laird of Pittencrieff may have become the embodiment of rank and wealth but nothing ever compared in grandeur to Pittencrieff itself.    Lauder had one commanding rule on these trips. His 'pupils', when it came to places celebrated in Scottish literature, were required as a preliminary, to master the writings that had made them famous. In accordance with this principle, Carnegie never saw Loch Katrine or the Trossachs which were only fifty miles from his home until he had read the 'Lady of The Lake' and committed large stretches of it to memory.

To Carnegie, the great Scottish rebel William Wallace, whom uncle Lauder endowed in their imagination, became the symbol of everything noble in human nature.  Carnegie recorded:

*"It was from uncle Lauder that I learned all that I know of the early history of Scotland, of Wallace, Bruce and Burns . . . I can truly say in the words of Burns that there was there and then created in me a vein of Scottish patriotism which will cease to exist only with life."*

When Carnegie once came heartbroken to his uncle Lauder to report that he had been told at school that England was much larger than Scotland. *"Not at all Naig,"* Lauder reassured him. *"'If Scotland were rolled out as flat as England, then Scotland would be much larger; but would you have the Highlands rolled down?"*

In time, conditions became so bad for the Carnegies in Dunfermline that Mrs Carnegie wrote to her two sisters in Pittsburgh in America suggesting the possibility of joining them "for the sake of the children."  Following much deliberation it was decided to sell the looms and furniture by auction and move to America. Carnegie never forgot the sweetness in his father's voice when he sang to the family:

*"To the West. to the West, to the land of the free,*
*Where the mighty Missouri rolls down to the sea;*
*Where a man is a man even though he must toil*
*And the poorest may gather the fruits of the soil."*

The sale of their personal goods never even brought enough to cover the cost of the journey. They were still twenty pounds short of the fare. However, a kind friend loaned the Carnegies the twenty pounds and with uncle Lauder agreeing to pay the 'good friend' back they were all set for the biggest gamble of their lives. Lauder offered them generous advice and took care of all of the details for their journey.

On the 17th May 1848, William Carnegie, forty three years of age, Margaret Carnegie, thirty three, Andrew, twelve and a half and Tom five, left the parish of Dunfermline for America. As the Carnegies climbed aboard the coal railroad omnibus that took them to Charleston, young Carnegie had felt very sad and, through tearful eyes, looked long and hard out of the window until the grand and sacred old Abbey and his beloved parish of Dunfermline vanished from view. The family were rowed over in a small boat to a waiting steamer in the Firth of Forth. As Carnegie was about to be taken from the small boat to the steamer he made a rush for his Uncle Lauder and clung round his neck, crying out: *"I canna leave ye! I canna leave ye!"* Eventually he was taken from Lauder by a kind sailor who lifted him onto the deck of the steamer.

Before the voyage to America the only journey Carnegie had ever experienced had been a day trip to Edinburgh to see the Queen. Uncle Lauder had taken his son George and young Carnegie across the River Forth for a view of the youthful 22 year old sovereign Queen Victoria while she made a celebrated visit to Edinburgh. Both boys were unimpressed. *"She's no sae tall as yer mither,"* said young George. *"Aye and her dress is nae sae braw either,"* replied young Carnegie, looking at his mother who had accompanied them in her best clothes.

With Lauder as the catalyst Carnegie, now about to embark on a journey of far reaching experience and consequence, had become a self educated young man. From the time he entered Lauder's back shop for his first years of formal and informal training, Carnegie had developed a thirst for education, knowledge and understanding which never ceased. He read constantly, he remembered what he read, and he was not at all hesitant about expressing opinions either in discussion or writing. In his memoirs Carnegie wrote that: *"I had left school forever, with the exception of one winter's night-schooling in America, and later a French night-teacher for a time, and, strange to say, an elocutionist from whom I learned how to declaim. I could read, write and cipher, and had begun the study of algebra and Latin."*

During the voyage to America Carnegie found comfort in writing heartfelt letters to his uncle Lauder in a style which was descriptive and profound. In later years he would seek out those who could teach him more, like Matthew Arnold, Herbert Spencer and John Morely, and learn from them in the way he had done from George Lauder.

Carnegie's great strengths throughout his life in pushing towards his goals were his quick adaptability and his eagerness to learn, even at the expense of having long held ideas shaken or his established procedures rendered obsolete. However, even with these strengths Carnegie was always torn between the two great influences of his childhood. There was the influence of the true idealism of justice, democracy and the rights of the people, as characterised by George Lauder and Tom Morrison, and the dominating force of his mother, aggressive, materialistic and determined to succeed. So that throughout Carnegie's life there is an internal conflict and tension between conserving the idealism of his radical family past and his determination to get to the very top. To Margaret Carnegie, George Lauder, who had married her sister, symbolised her view of success. After all he lived and owned a business on the High Street of Dunfermline.

In the early days Mrs Carnegie kept body and soul together earning four dollars a week mending shoes: *"Her eye beamed keen with honour"* said Carnegie. Meanwhile William Carnegie struggled from door to door trying to sell unwanted cloths.

Once in America Andrew Carnegie wasted no time in looking for work and managed to get a job as a bobbin boy in a textile mill earning one dollar twenty a week. After numerous sleepless nights having nightmares about the boiler being too high he badly desired a change of occupation but was far too proud of his contribution to the family income to do anything about it. However, as luck would have it, the boss, a Scotsman by the name of John Hay was in need of a clerk. He had asked Carnegie for a demonstration of his writing and counting skills in order to keep books for him.

With the confidence and education gained from his Uncle Lauder and "Snuffy Martin", Carnegie obliged to the satisfaction of his employer. Hay kept his books on a single entry system until Carnegie, forever listening and forever learning, found out that most of the big firms kept their books in double entry.

As a consequence, Carnegie turned to education once again and attended night school in Pittsburgh during the winter of 1849 to learn double entry book-keeping. During that same year Andrew was offered a job that made him "wild with delight" working as a telegraph messenger boy for the O'Reilly Telegraph Company. Carnegie became one of the first people in America to be able to decipher telegraph messages by ear and thus became a celebrity within Pittsburgh because of this self taught skill. Excited and optimistic Carnegie had to tell his uncle Lauder about his new life in America: "Although I would like to be back in Dunfermline … it is far better for me that I came here … In Dunfermline I would have been a poor weaver all my days, but here I can surely do something better than that. If I don't it will be all my own fault, for anyone can get along in this country."

In the early 1850s he met a man who was from the same caring mould as George Lauder. Thomas A Scott, Superintendent of the Railroads Western Division, noticed Carnegie as a bright and cheerful telegraph messenger boy and was keen to employ him. Scott, like Lauder in Scotland, was to have a big influence on Carnegie's young adult life. From stoking a boiler in a dark cellar to the wide-open sunshine, and with an increase in pay to thirty-five dollars a month, Carnegie secured the one break that was to change the course of his life. In 1853 he became Scott's assistant and telegraph messenger on the Pennsylvania Railroad. He pursued his new job with the same hunger and passion shown in the back shop of Uncle Lauder's grocery business in Dunfermline. Every day Carnegie learned new street names and, every day and some evenings, he could be seen carrying books around with him borrowed from the 'Colonel James Anderson' free library in Pittsburgh, which he would read between delivering messages.

Books which gave Carnegie a taste for literature and would otherwise have been impossible for him to have obtained elsewhere were, by the generosity of Colonel Anderson's Library, within his reach. Not only did Carnegie have a monument built to the memory of the Colonel but the wisdom of the deed itself was never forgotten by Carnegie who later endowed free libraries as a way of spreading "sweetness and light" to those less fortunate. "The fundamental advantage of a library", wrote Carnegie, "is that it gives nothing for nothing; youths must acquire knowledge themselves; there is no escape from this."

During these early years in America Carnegie, still clinging to his Dunfermline roots, saw himself carrying on uncle Lauder's egalitarian crusade by organising a debating society to debate such issues as *"Should the judiciary be elected by the people?"* In 1852, Carnegie, in another of his letters to his uncle Lauder, demonstrated his maturity and statesmanship by giving Lauder a flavour of the general situation in his new country:

*"...You would laugh to see how they [the politicians] have to bow to their sovereigns the people. ...Slavery, I hope, will soon be abolished in this country"* and *"...there is much excitement here upon the subject of Temperance. The state of Maine passed a law prohibiting the manufacture or sale, except for medical purposes, of all intoxicating liquors; several states have passed similar laws."*

On 2nd October 1855, Carnegie's father, William, died and his death left Andrew Carnegie to manage all the domestic affairs to a greater extent than ever.

With the help of Tom Scott, Carnegie began to learn the complexities of railroads which had become America's largest industry. Carnegie soon worked his way up to a position of responsibility within the telegraph office occasionally looking after things when the manager was out. He also worked with Scott and helped him to develop larger and longer locomotives to carry fuller loads and to help him to cut costs. They were the first in America to keep telegraph stations open and the trains moving twenty four hours a day. Carnegie learned from Scott what made their Railroad a model for the whole of America, by keeping costs down and by running them full and fast.

As the Railroad expanded, Scott taught Carnegie how they could make a profit along the line. In 1856 Scott advised Carnegie to purchase shares in the Adams Express company (a forerunner of American Express). In 1858 Scott secured a small share in a company making sleeping cars for the railroad companies for his young protégé. Young Carnegie borrowed the 1,250 dollars from the bank for his investment, but it was quickly repaid from the dividends he received. By 1860 this investment in sleeping cars had secured Carnegie an annual income of 5,000 dollars. Carnegie called it: *"the goose that laid the golden eggs".* From then on Carnegie was forever on the lookout for new investments.

Andrew Carnegie at twenty-four.

As a result of their instability, he saw the need to replace wooden bridges with iron ones and formed a company to make them. His investments had soon become so profitable that his salary of twenty four hundred dollars a year was merely five per cent of his income.

In 1861 the American Civil War broke out and Carnegie became a part of the war effort along with Mr Scott, who had been appointed Assistant Secretary of War in charge of the Transportation Division. As Carnegie had charge of the telegraph department as well as the railways it gave him an opportunity of meeting with the great and the good like Abraham Lincoln who would come to the telegraph office to await replies to telegrams and for information. According to Carnegie, *"his manners were perfect because they were natural."*

In 1862 Carnegie was struck down with illness and was granted leave of absence by the Pennsylvania Railroad Company. At age twenty seven he made his first long awaited visit back to Scotland in June of that year. While travelling from Liverpool to Dunfermline, Carnegie felt that he was in a dream and both he and his mother could hardly contain their excitement. Carnegie's love for Dunfermline had not waned. If anything, it had grown even stronger: *"I felt as if I could throw myself upon the sacred soil and kiss it"* he said.

By the time he reached his Scottish home at Uncle Lauder's house and went into the old room where Lauder had taught him and Dod, he could not help but notice how small everything looked compared to what he had imagined. The High Street, which he had considered to be like Broadway, uncle Lauder's shop which he had compared to some New York establishments, and the height of the houses, had all shrunk. The schoolhouse around which had centred many of his schoolboy recollections and the playground upon which mimic battles had been fought and races run, had shrunk into ridiculously small dimensions. He described the town as: *"A city of Lilliputians."*

However, Carnegie's description of his Uncle Lauder did not enter this laughable equation: *"My home, of course, was with my instructor, guide, and inspirer, George Lauder; he who had done so much to make me romantic, patriotic and poetical at eight. Now I was twenty-seven, but Uncle Lauder still remained Uncle Lauder. He had not shrunk, no one could fill his place. We had our walks and talks constantly and I was Naig again to him. He never had any name for me but that and never did have. My dear, dear uncle, and more, much more than an uncle to me."*

While staying at Lauder's house Carnegie caught a cold which developed into a fever and he was laid up in bed for six weeks, at times in a critical condition. This illness eventually put an end to Carnegie's Scottish visit and, though sad to leave Dunfermline, he was happy to get back to the warm American climate.

In 1864, American railway lines were in much demand and this attracted Carnegie to move into the business of making rails. His investments began to require so much of his personal attention that he decided to leave the railway company and concentrate on his own affairs. He left the Pennsylvania Railroad a year later and though he was by now a fairly wealthy man he was still far from being satisfied.

In 1866, as a result of a great demand for locomotives, Andrew Carnegie and Thomas N Miller launched the Pittsburgh Locomotive Works which became famous throughout the United States and, for one of the two partners, yet another very prosperous concern.

In 1868, at the age of thirty-three, Carnegie made a promise to himself to work only two more years, to educate himself and then to devote his life to good causes: *"Simply making more money would degrade me beyond permanent recovery"* he wrote. It was a strange form of self righteousness which reflected the philosophy of his own father who spoke the language of altruism and the philosophy of his Uncle Lauder who championed the cause of an egalitarian society.

Carnegie's manufacturing business was hardly able to keep the demands of the American public satisfied fast enough. His cousin Dod (Mr George Lauder Jr) whom Carnegie had corresponded with since leaving Scotland in 1848, and who eventually went to work with his cousin as a partner, developed a new kind of system for Carnegie's mill operations, which transformed the mill from merely efficient to super-efficient overnight. Lauder introduced the process of washing and cooking the old dross from coal mines, which had until then been thrown away as waste material.

Like Carnegie, young George Lauder had graduated from his father's back shop to become a mechanical engineer at Glasgow University. As a result of his knowledge, they secured contracts from the leading coal companies for all of their old dross and young Lauder superintended the construction of the first coal-washing machinery in America. The coal companies thought them insane but that suited Lauder's and Carnegie's purposes.

The ovens were extended until they had five hundred of them washing nearly five hundred tons of coal daily. To Carnegie, cousin Lauder, who had produced superior coke from material that had been for years thrown over the side as worthless, was proving himself to be one of many assets of Carnegie's growing business.

Carnegie, at thirty-three, had an annual income of fifty thousand dollars. Even at this stage of his life he was still holding dear the advice given from his Uncle Lauder to continue learning all through life: *"I will resign business at thirty-five, but during the ensuing two years I wish to spend the afternoons in receiving instruction and in reading systematically."*

All his capital was now in manufacturing and as the Carnegie empire expanded he was compelled to mass produce wrought iron to make the bridges for the trains to travel on. As such he thought it prudent to manufacture his own pig iron. Always looking after the pennies, Carnegie became suspicious of the levels of iron in the ore he was buying to make the pig iron and hit on the idea of hiring a chemist who had it analysed for iron content. The result was that ironstone from mines with a reputation for having a high ore content was proved to be false. With this knowledge at his disposal Carnegie's iron furnace became the most profitable part of the business.

Carnegie had not failed to notice the steady growth of the new Bessemer Steel production and how this new process was taking over from Iron. With the move from iron to the production of steel, Carnegie was now to embark on the most profitable venture of his business empire.

His steel-rail company was formed in 1873 with an initial order of 2,000 steel rails for the Pennsylvania Railroad. He surprised a meeting of mill owners who had divided the rail market among them by demanding a share equal to the largest. He had bought stock in all of their companies and having read their reports was able to announce that he knew his costs and he also knew theirs. If they refused to give him the share that he was asking for then, in effect, he would run them all out of business because they could not compete with him.

His competitors would study profits while Carnegie would concentrate on costs, keeping them as low as possible and tracking them hour by hour, penny by penny. Competition was his driving force but it drove his workforce twelve hours a day seven days a week, the fourth of July being the only holiday they were ever allowed. As the Industrial Revolution had claimed the jobs of handloom weavers, like his father back in Dunfermline, it was now claiming the jobs of the skilled craftsmen like the old "Puddlers" who had for generations controlled the process of making wrought iron in small batches. With the Bessemer steel process Carnegie had introduced a scale of production which had not only revolutionised working practices, but had revolutionised America itself. It was an irreversible shift of industrialisation and mass production which fuelled the growth of the American nation.

The steel industry, which Carnegie was now dominating, symbolised America's new national and technological superiority. *"Steel had ascended the throne and was driving away all inferior material"* said Carnegie.

In one of numerous journeys to Scotland in 1881, Carnegie was able to keep a promise which he had given to his mother, Margaret, to ride in a coach and return successfully to Dunfermline which they had fled in poverty thirty-three years earlier. With Carnegie at the reins and his mother seated on top, the coach rolled passed the old wonderland of privilege at Pittencrieff Glen, closed by the Laird to Carnegie when only a boy, and up the High Street which had been decorated to welcome Andrew who had just donated a Library, his first of many world library donations, to his native town. The coach stopped in front of George Lauder's shop, their destination for the next few weeks, and where Andrew could once again join in the company of his beloved tutor and mentor, Uncle Lauder.

The architect of the library asked Carnegie what motto he had wanted above the library door. Carnegie, remembering his father's attempts to found a library in Dunfermline in the early 1800s and his uncle Lauder's constant emphasis on education, asked for the rising sun shedding its rays to be carved with the motto: *"Let there be light."*

In 1886 Carnegie's mother and brother died suddenly within a few days of each other while he lay in bed unable to move with typhoid fever. He never knew of their deaths until he had made a full recovery. When he was told, he was devastated. His one ray of comfort was that he was now free to court and marry his sweetheart Louise Whitfield which he did on 22nd April 1887. They spent their honeymoon on the Isle of Wight and, with his mother, father and brother now departed, Carnegie invited his closest relative and friend George Lauder to be with them for the happy occasion.

They travelled to Dunfermline where Carnegie delighted in showing his new wife the haunts and incidents of his youth and where his Uncle Lauder had taken him into his heart and taught him so many things.
Carnegie's profits by the late eighteen hundreds were three million dollars per

year, four million in 1894 and they continued to rise year after year. Many of his partners, including his cousin George Lauder, began suggesting dividends, but no dividends were even considered because Carnegie continued to re-invest every penny of profit. He secured a huge source of cheap iron ore and invested in lake boats to bring the ore through the great lakes. He built his own railroads to haul the ore from the shores of Lake Erie to Pittsburgh and managed to reduce the price of rails from twenty eight dollars a ton to as low as fourteen dollars a ton. His competitors were both amazed and demoralised.

By 1899 Carnegie had set a very high standard for the American industry, producing more steel than the whole of the entire steel industry of the United Kingdom. He was now standing on the peak of total triumph in his own field and was planning for a life of philanthropy and of putting into practice his own 'gospel of wealth'.

In October 1899, as part of George Lauder's endless efforts to secure meaningful technical education and Carnegie's gospel of wealth, Fife was about to secure a technical school that would be the pride of Fife and would put it in the vanguard of education in Scotland.

27 July 1881 Andrew Carnegie arrived by coach with his mother to lay the memorial stone for the first 'Carnegie Free Library'. The coach is situated outside George Lauder's house.

Margaret Carnegie was the sister-in law of George Lauder. Lauder had married her sister Seaton Morrison in 1835.

The first of many libraries gifted by Andrew Carnegie to his native town.
George Lauder and Andrew Carnegie's father William were founder's of the Dunfermline Library long before this grand building was erected.

From humble beginnings to symbols of wealth. Skibo Castle, for many years the home of Andrew Carnegie. It was here that the portrait of Carnegie's old uncle, George Lauder, hung with pride until it was gifted to the College in 1965 by Carnegie's daughter, Margaret. (DPL LHC)

Andrew Carnegie with Wife Louise and Daughter Margaret.

Andrew Carnegie became Rector of St Andrews University in 1906.
In this painting by H R Butler, Carnegie looks every inch the protege
of his uncle George Lauder.

# Lauder Technical School

*"When I found myself at the age of twenty five at the back of a counter with a deficient education for the trade I had engaged in, I resolved that every youth that came under my influence would get a good technical and literary education."*

George Lauder

*"Education gives a man, who really absorbs it, higher tastes and aims than just the acquisition of wealth, and a world to enjoy, into which the mere millionaire cannot enter . . ."*

Andrew Carnegie

At first glance the year 1899 seems an unlikely year in which history would care to record any aspect of education for posterity. It marked the end of a century which had crept in with an 'Act' of humanity in the shape of the formal abolition of slavery, raced through the decades on the rollercoaster of the Industrial Revolution and ended with acts of barbarity, against "stubborn" Dutch in the South African Boer War.

These events of great consequence were probably inconsequential in comparison with the more immediate problems for the people of Fife in securing a living in a fast changing, fast living society. Industry had been, and was being, revolutionised and was requiring a workforce that could keep pace with the rapid changes that were taking place.

According to one Scottish contemporary, Reverend J. Smith, it was necessary to approach the planning of education: *"as a business problem, demanding a business-like solution. Our system of education should be organised as if it were a business concern, in which all the parts are to be so ordered that each is considered only as it directly serves the definite end in view."*

With the 1872 Education Act, authority had finally managed to ignore the firmly held views that education of the poor was both unnecessary and dangerous and accepted in principle that it was in fact a 'good idea' if only to make them morally and physically good citizens.

It was against this backdrop of cynicism and narrow-mindedness that George Lauder had, in 1893, finally resigned in the face of mounting opposition to his ideas from the School Board to pursue the campaign for free and technical education for all. Lauder had been a pioneer and had never been afraid to blaze an unknown trail even to the extent of courting unpopularity. The final straw was a petition which was hawked through the streets of West Fife in opposition to the building of a new school for technical education.

Following George Lauder's resignation from the School Board, in which he had worked energetically for technical education, he began working even harder outside of the Board for a vision which would meet the needs of both the community and industry.

On 17th September 1897, Mr Andrew Burt, Chairman of the Burgh School Board, received a letter from Mr George Lauder, Park Avenue, stating that he had been authorised by one who was a true friend of Dunfermline and well-wisher of its educational advantage to say that he was prepared to lay out a sum of £7,000 for the building and resourcing of a technical school in the town of Dunfermline. The true friend of Dunfermline and well wisher of education was non other than Andrew Carnegie. Two days later the Board met and unanimously agreed to accept the offer contained in Mr Lauder's letter. On it being found afterwards that the cost of the school would exceed £7,000, Mr Carnegie increased his offer to £10,000 and later again to £13,000.

Carnegie's agreement to fund his uncle's vision for education made strange reading coming from a man who only began formal schooling at age eight, leaving just five years later at age thirteen. Carnegie built up a mass of material on the subject of education for life as well as for the acquisition of wealth and had been kept informed of his uncle's efforts and ideas to secure free and meaningful technical education in his native town. Education was one of Carnegie's pet subjects and, although he never once complained in public of his own sparse formal tuition, he never missed an opportunity of letting the world know of his own educational debt of gratitude to his uncle and mentor, George Lauder.

A grand view of old Lauder Technical School next to the even older Dunfermline High School taken about the turn of the century. In the foreground children are seen coming and going from one school to the other. (DPL LHC)

It was decided that Lauder Technical School would be built on the site next to the old Dunfermline High School in Priory Lane. The road along Priory Lane had been widened by twelve feet and a granolithic pavement laid from the houses on the north side of the street along to the entrance to the schools for easier access.

Lauder Technical School was built from plans prepared by the Glasgow architect Messrs H & D Barclay, the same architect who drew up the plans for the Dunfermline High School and for the reconstructed Commercial School. Lauder Technical School was regarded by many as one of the finest technical schools in the whole country, using the finest local labour and materials from their own doorstep:-

Mason - Mr J Stewart, Dunfermline
Joiner - Mr J Westwood, Dunfermline
Plasterer - Messrs H & D Ramsay, Dunfermline
Plumber - Rolland & Co, Dunfermline
Gas Fittings - Messrs J Inglis & Son, Dunfermline
Gas Engine - Tangyes, Ltd, Glasgow and Birmingham
Electrical Engineers - Anderson & Nimmo, Glasgow
Mechanical Engineers - A Bennett & Son, Dunfermline
Heating - Ritchie & Co., Edinburgh

Of three floors in height, the building was well adapted for the higher grade teaching recognised as commercially necessary for Scotland to hold its own in manufacturing and other competitive industries. The lower floor was occupied by two workshops, an engine-room and space occupied by mechanical ventilation and heating.

The larger workshop, 70 feet by 30 feet, was fitted up for manual instruction in wood working with benches and lathes and drawing desks where the exercises to be worked out with tools were first drafted onto paper. The other workshop was for instruction in metalwork in connection with the drawing classes in engineering and mining.

On the first floor there was a workshop equipped with two powerlooms and six handlooms. Even though handloom weaving had taken a tumble it was still a very popular industry around Fife. It was never intended that the weavers were to be taught their trade, only that those who may have been proposing to be designers could have a knowledge of how designs were carried out. The same practical studies were also available to those who were seeking to be clerks or commercially connected with the manufacture or sale of textile goods. Designs in a range of fabrics were drawn out and woven and a collection of the best and most novel examples were held as part of a small museum. Other accommodation on the first floor was a large apartment 70 feet by 30 feet, capable of being divided into three separate classrooms by folding doors. These rooms were for mechanical engineering and mining engineering drawing classes. This floor also held a physical laboratory and apparatus room (gymnasium).

A small lift conveyed apparatus to lecture rooms on the upper floor. This upper floor also held a chemical laboratory where materials for experiments were made ready and passed to the lecture hall for use.

A fully equipped Art school with rooms for object drawing, cast and antique drawing and a room for modelling in clay completed the accommodation on the upper floor. These art rooms were very effectively lit from the north and east by a large single sheet of glass so that no extraneous shadows were cast upon the models.

Power for the new Lauder Technical School was provided for in the basement by an 18 horsepower gas Tangye engine which drove the electric dynamo, a 72 inch ventilating fan, several turning lathes for metal and wood, grindstone, saw and powerlooms. The fittings in each department were specially designed to meet the requirements of the teaching needs of the various sections.

Lauder Technical School was the first technical school in Fife to have mechanical ventilation installed as part of the building. The air was passed through a horse hair screen, upon which water was allowed to run and the air was delivered through a subway in which were deposited coils of hot water pipes turning into every classroom in the building, air being discharged into the room about eight feet above the floor.

Whilst the rooms were being heated, ceiling ventilators would be closed and the heated air would fill up the rooms from the ceiling downwards. This process was reversed in summertime.

The School Board had the assistance of Dr John Macdonald, Rector of the Dunfermline High School, who laboured all through his holidays to arrange the classes for the inauguration.

The opening ceremony took place in the largest room on the first floor of the new school on Tuesday 10th October 1899. Long before the appointed hour of three o'clock, this room was filled to capacity with around 600 people from all over the country eager to hear the speakers and to witness history in the making. There was little sign of the thunder and vivid flashes of lightning and continuous heavy rain which had fallen all the previous day and night.

The storm, which had come in violent gusts from the east, melted into the background as the ceremony got underway.

It was arranged that the Right Hon the Earl of Elgin K.G, Secretary of State for the Colonies, would take the chair and that Mr Andrew Carnegie, the man who had endowed the school, would be one of the principal speakers. On the stroke of three o'clock, the Earl of Elgin, Lady Louisa Bruce, Mr and Mrs Carnegie, Mr George Lauder and Miss Lauder and party, along with members of the Dunfermline School Board and others, drove up to the door of the new Technical School. They were met by a throng of pupils from the neighbouring High School who had lined the walk and sang three cheers on the arrival of the dignitaries.

Lord Elgin opened the proceedings by saying that he could not help but remember a similar occasion thirteen years earlier when he was invited to take part in the opening of the High School next door to the new technical school. He felt gratified to be called on once again to welcome what he called "this sister institution" which had now come to share in the great work of education.

*"None of Mr Carnegie's numerous gifts is more full of promise,"* said Lord Elgin, *"than this new technical school which today he is to dedicate to one of the greatest of all causes - namely, the provision of greater intellectual culture."* He went on, *"I find that during my five years absence from this country the introduction of the bicycle has brought about such a revolution in the means and manner of locomotion that I don't think it too much to say that there is hardly a village, or even a house that is not accessible to the new school."* Lord Elgin concluded by saying, *" . . . may I express my good wishes to those to whom the management of this good ship is now to be entrusted; hoping that they may find favourable winds and smooth seas, full cargoes and - perhaps I may say, cheap freights."*

Mr Andrew Carnegie, who was received with great applause, was next to speak:

*" . . .Our noble chairman has been good enough to point to me as the agent through whom this institution has been secured for my native town."* Carnegie said to a hushed audience; *"Believe me ladies and gentlemen, I am unable to accept that position. There is one man - another man - who is entitled to the credit. A man who has stood as an advocate of technical education through good report and through evil report. A man whose devotion to that cause, whose enthusiasm inspired his nephew. I simply wrote a few words on a sheet of paper and our good friend Mr Ross got his bank*

to take that piece of paper, and this school rose like Aladdin's Palace. I had only to rub the ring . . . to my uncle belongs the credit. He bore aloft the lamp. He devoted years of his time and his thought to this purpose, while I did all I had to do in a minute. It is not he who gives the money who is the real giver - money that he never misses. No, it is the man who gives his heart to the work. What my uncle did you do not know. I cannot trust myself to begin to tell you what that man has been, not only to me, but to many other young men. I look back upon his record from my childhood until now, when he has in his old age, the love and the obedience of friends all over. He has been right upon every public question and has been on picket duty in the great army of progress. Perhaps so far ahead of the main army that he ran the risk of being shot."

Carnegie spoke of his uncle Lauder with great fondness of memory:

"I can remember uncle Lauder rehearsing a speech in his back shop in Dunfermline, which was to electrify an audience in connection with the Corn Law agitation. Uncle Lauder was right then. He was right with the Crimean War - not popular, but right.

Any man can be popular who advocates war. No man can be popular who advocates peace until the records are made up, passions are passed, and the reign of peace returns.

My uncle was also right on the American Union question. I am delighted to see that the American Union is now such a tremendous customer for linen goods manufactured in my native town. My uncle was right in connection with the American Union; he stood up for liberty - for freedom against slavery; and he was right on the question of water. But the last and greatest cause fortunate enough to enlist his enthusiasm was in technical education.

Let me tell you! he put his finger on the weak spot of this Empire of Great Britain - the lack of just that, technical education.

Now, I have a wish lying very near to my heart. It is not a new wish. It is one that was born the day that I said to my uncle, you book me to take £10,000 to build this school; and it is this.

I wish to ask nothing in regard to this school; I never interfere with any gift that I give. I believe in strict home rule. But it would give me, and it would give Mrs Carnegie, genuine pleasure if you would approve of calling this technical school the "LAUDER Technical School."

The appeal was met by thunderous applause from the audience, many of whom had been opposed to the idea only six years previous. George Lauder's quiet demeanour was to give way to shock and surprise as his nephew made the impassioned appeal.

*"I judge by your applause that this commends itself to you"* said the smiling Carnegie. *"It seems like asking an honour for myself, because I have never been able to dissociate myself from my uncle, who is part of us, but if this is not asking too much I beg to ask it at the hands of the authorities of Dunfermline so that the name of the man who was really the spirit which produced this school may go down in your annals for ever as a citizen who in his day and generation has done the town some service."*

That Carnegie should calculate this occasion to express publicly the private gratitude and deep respect which he had long held for George Lauder was of great significance. It presented him with the first real opportunity of letting the public know and also of letting uncle Lauder know, the high esteem in which he held Lauder as a man as well as the uncle of the small boy who made good. The ties of kinship and education with which the two great men were bound was for its time so taken for granted that it was difficult to grasp a clear impression of its tremendous importance.

George Lauder, now eighty-four years of age, had been labouring under some emotion when he was called upon to say a few words. He made a brave attempt to address the audience but was forced to hand over his notes to Mr William Robertson, local manufacturer, to read on his behalf as the full realisation of what Carnegie had said set in.

Mr Robertson began by explaining the situation to the audience:

*"My Lord, Mr and Mrs Carnegie, ladies and gentlemen, I feel sure it is with regret that we have to recognise the fact that the burden of years prevents our friend Mr Lauder from fulfilling completely the part assigned to him today. That he is one of Dunfermline's grand old men we will all admit. I confess I feel honoured not only in being allowed to do him this little service, but in being permitted to take this humble part in a function so interesting in itself, and in connection with building that which will contribute, I am certain, in very great degree to the mental and material progress of our old city. I will now read Mr Lauder's speech."*

"Ladies and gentlemen, I am delighted to be here today at the opening of this Technical College . .
." Lauder never once referred to the technical school as a school but always as a College. ". . . an institution which I am certain will do much for the future welfare of the youth of Dunfermline and Fife. It is a difficult matter to speak of so as to make my views interesting, but you will forgive me referring to my own education and the part I have taken in educational affairs in our town.

It is 72 years ago since I was taught in my father's snuff mill at the bottom of Hunt's Glen the use of saw and chisel, of brace and bit.

That was the Technical Education I had, and it was very good of its kind, and long before the too common phrase "Made in Germany" was heard of. I always look back with satisfaction on having been taught thus early the use of my hands.

It is nearly 50 years since Mr Simpson, an advocate from Edinburgh was brought to lecture on free education from the school to the university, and I had, I am happy to say, a hand in bringing him here to plead for a scheme which I would like to live to see realised completely. Things have certainly advanced in this direction, and advanced pretty far, and my hope is that this fine College will be so managed as to be an example to other communities, and help forward that noble plan of free education throughout all Scotland.

I was four times elected to the School Board, and during all my terms of office I was a persistent advocate of technical education, because I knew that the knowledge I had got from the use of tools had made me a kind of handy man through life. When I found myself at the age of 25 at the back of a counter with a deficient education for the trade I had got engaged in, I resolved that every youth that came under my influence would get a good technical and literary training. I could mention my influences whom I have assisted in this way, but I will speak only of two - one my son, George Lauder, and the other my nephew, Andrew Carnegie. When they were boys they assisted me in business, Burns works lay open in my back shop and I taught them to recite his poems, and poured into their veins a love of Wallace, Bruce, Burns and old Scotland.

Many other things I spoke to them about that were then thought nothing of at school; but why do I mention these things? It is for this reason, namely, that it is on account of that very training I have been speaking of that Dunfermline has got this splendid College. Mr Carnegie has said so himself to me, and I am proud to repeat it. In short I ask our good town frankly if we have done this for Dunfermline, what is Dunfermline going to do for itself?

... What I say is, that we are entitled to ask that this College shall be made free to all scholars in the district who are proved to be capable of benefiting by its education and training.

My own idea is that it should be free to all pupils who have obtained the merit certificate. I advance this because a change of school at this stage would introduce them to new teachers and new subjects, and bring them more fully prepared to evening school - a school of more importance to many than the day school.

I have in my possession letters from Mr Beverage of Linlithgow and Mr Hardie of Leith, giving me full information of their technical and secondary schools being free schools.

Leith rates are 1s 2d, and no complaints - our rates last year were 9d. We have in Dunfermline at and below £9 of rent 3999 ratepayers, and their average payment per year is 2s, half of which is paid by the landlord. Surely this is a small payment for free education for a family. Twopence per £ additional, and this would make the secondary school and the new College free to all in all time coming. Then no man could say that the new College is not a place for his children."

As Mr Robertson took his seat the whole place erupted with thunderous applause.

Mr Lauder had one duty to perform before he was finished. He opened a blue plush case containing a magnificent and elegantly designed solid gold key. Addressing the chairman of the School Board he said: "Mr Burt it is a proud day for me when I can hand you the key of such a Technical College as this for my native town."

On one side of the key, under the presentation of the city arms, was the following description: "The key of Lauder Technical School, Dunfermline, opened 10th October, 1899, the Right Hon. Earl of Elgin presiding." On the other side, surmounted by a thistle, was the drawing: "Built by the munificence of Andrew Carnegie, Esq., of Skibo, and presented as a memorial to his uncle, George Lauder, Esq., to the School Board of the burgh of Dunfermline."

In accepting the gift of the gold key to the new Lauder Technical School Mr Andrew Burt, Chairman of the School Board, read out the contents of an address to Mr Carnegie which had been agreed by the School Board:

Sir,

The School Board of the burgh of Dunfermline thankfully accept the gift of the Lauder Technical School which you have now presented to them through the medium of your friend Mr George Lauder.

In accepting the gift they desire to assure you that they realise the responsibility which is imposed upon them and they pledge themselves to hold the school as dedicated to the benefit of succeeding generations of the youth of Dunfermline, and therefore as a sacred trust which it becomes them to administer to with fidelity and direction.

The School Board desire to avail themselves of the opportunity offered by your presence, along with Mrs Carnegie, at the opening of the school, to express their high appreciation of your deep interest in the cause of education. They have special pleasure and pride in recognising that a native of their town is so widely known and honoured throughout Great Britain and America enlightened with liberal efforts to promote the diffusion of knowledge.

They feel assured that your name will, by the people of both countries be long and gratefully cherished for your many beneficence, they desire to express the hope that you may be long spared to witness the fruits of that wider diffusion of knowledge which you have done so much to promote.

In the name of the School Board, &c.,

Andrew Burt, Chairman.
Daniel Gorrie, Clerk.

In a personal capacity Mr Burt added:

". . . It is impossible Mr Carnegie could have bestowed a more acceptable or a more timely gift upon his native town. Within recent years there have been great changes in the policy of the Scotch Education Department . . . This building, which through the generosity and wise forethought of Mr Carnegie we have now been placed in possession of, will enable us to take advantage of those changes introduced by the Education Department and meet the growing wants of the community. We feel that the form in which we as a School Board and the community can best convey to Mr Carnegie our appreciation of this princely gift is by assuring him that the facilities which it affords will be taken advantage of to the fullest extent.

Mr Carnegie has expressed a desire that the name of George Lauder, his friend - and I think I may say, our friend - should be permanently associated with this building. To this desire the School Board most readily and cordially assent.

They recognise that after the name Carnegie no name could be more fittingly associated with this institution. They know that Mr Lauder has long taken a deep and warm interest in the cause of education, not only as a private citizen but for many years a member of our Board. They know that for long he has cherished a desire and a great hope to see an institution such as this established in our midst, and it must be to him today a matter of extreme gratification that through the liberality of his nephew he has seen the fulfilment of his long cherished hope."

Further speeches were made by such worthies as Sir Swire Smith, a member of the Royal Commission appointed by the Government several years previous to visit and report back on all the leading schools of the world, Mr John Ross, Convenor of the High School Committee, Mr D Gorrie, Clerk to the School Board, The Rev. Mr George, Convenor of the Technical Schools Committee, and the Rev. Robert Stevenson, who dedicated prayers for the new technical school.

The local newspapers were quick to report on the man who had made it all happen: "After the ceremony of the new Technical School on Tuesday," wrote the Dunfermline Journal, "it cannot be said that a prophet hath no honour in his own country. If any man in Dunfermline can claim to be a prophet, it is Mr George Lauder, and if any man has been honoured in this town, it is the self-same gentleman. The high eulogies passed upon him would have been no little honour in themselves; but over and above all praise bestowed, the new school has been christened the "Lauder Technical School" and Mr Lauder's name - to quote Mr Carnegie's own words — "will go down in our annals for ever as a citizen who in his day and generation did the town some service."

"It is fitting," said the Journal, "that Mr Lauder's name should be associated with the new school. He has certainly been a remarkable man - so remarkable indeed, that the proceedings on Tuesday were not without their humorous side. The dreamer and visionary of twenty years ago has lived through the opposition he had to encounter, and has been lauded as a far-seeing educational reformer, even by those who used to ridicule his peculiar notions. Although Mr Carnegie - speaking, no doubt out of the fullness of his heart - may have been somewhat lavish in his praise, the fact remains that, on the question of education, Mr Lauder has been before his time. High educational authorities of today have generally accepted the views he held sixteen or twenty years ago.

*These views were simply that education should be free, and that the instruction to be given should be on commercial and scientific lines with the great object of effectively training the young for the battles of life.*

*While Mr Lauder was before his time in the advocacy of commercial and technical education, he is still a long way ahead of, at least, the bulk of the people of Dunfermline. Mr Lauder exclaims – "if we have done this for Dunfermline (meaning, given it a Technical School) what is Dunfermline going to do for itself ?*

*What Mr Lauder would have it do is to put 2% on the rates, and make the High School and the Technical School "free for all in all time coming."*

The interest which surrounded the opening of the new Lauder Technical School impressed upon the people of Scotland the first real understanding that a great impetus had been given to secondary and technical education in Fife which was bold, imaginative, urgently required and progressive.

To George Lauder the new Technical School was the realisation of his vision and the manifestation of all of his efforts over the decades of hard work and campaigning for free and technical education. Lauder's flame had kindled the ardour in Carnegie and now through the Technical School he was about to kindle the flame in countless generations of others.

More importantly perhaps, to industry and the communities of Fife, the new Lauder Technical School meant that at last meaningful and accessible education would now be available as a first step towards social, economic and industrial progress for the next one hundred years and beyond.

George Lauder (circa 1875) was overcome with emotion when his nephew, Andrew Carnegie, asked the Dunfermline School Board, on 10 October 1899, if they would do him the honour of naming the new technical school 'Lauder' Technical School, after his uncle Lauder.

One of the earliest photographs ever taken of Dr John MacDonald, first Rector of the new Lauder Technical School. Here Dr MacDonald is seated front row centre along with fifteen other of his Lauder Technical School staff. It is very likely that the soon to be appointed first headmaster of Lauder, Mr John Robertson, is seated to the right of Dr MacDonald: circa 1902. (DPL LHC)

# The Early Years

While the community of Dunfermline in the mid 1800s had comprised mainly church-going, radical handloom weavers, with coal-mining taking place on the northern and western outskirts of the town, the early years of the twentieth century brought considerable changes to industry and exploited new links with the south following the opening of the new Forth Rail Bridge in 1890.

In January 1900, the new century began for one woman at the Burgh Police Court. Elizabeth Thomson, euphemistically described as a "vagrant" was charged with "neglect" for exposing her child of tender years to severe and stormy weather while they huddled down for the night in Bothwell Street, Dunfermline. Both were clad in old rags and were shivering with cold and hunger. She was sent to prison for fourteen days.   On the wilder side of Fife, David McFeat, Carter, was given the option in January 1900 of being fined ten shillings or serving seven days imprisonment for being helplessly drunk and in charge of a horse and cart.

David McEwan found himself in court on a charge of 'Wife Assault'. It was stated that in the home of him and his wife, he struck her (wife) on the head with a poker. McEwan said that, "he merely touched her after she had thrown a stool at him." McEwan promised to behave himself and was let off with a five shillings fine. Meanwhile, young Mary McQueen, millworker, pled guilty at Cupar Sheriff Court on a charge of theft. She was sent to prison for one week.

On the political side, the Parliamentary Roll for one part of Fife had been made up but still required to be approved by the Sheriff. However, a lady's name had slipped into the roll and this had disturbed the equanimity of both the Conservatives and Liberals. The official agents of both parties protested vehemently at such an outrage. "Frances" was thus struck off the roll. On the industrial front the situation was not always progressive. Yet another pit accident occurred in a Fife colliery where young 17 year old William Clark had both his legs crushed and had to be carried up the pit in severe pain. He was put into the Coal Companies rubbish cart and taken home. Unfortunately the weather was foul with wind and rain which only added to the boy's misfortune.

Also the ambulance wagon, while available, had no horses owing to their requirement for other work at the pit.

This was the scene around Fife following the opening of the Lauder Technical School, the first in its field in the old Kingdom. It was also notable in having been recognised through the Scotch Education Department for what may have been the first training course for schoolmasters and teachers with a view to the introduction of technical education in schools.

Technical instruction was carried on under the auspices of local committees recognised by the Science and Art Department, South Kensington, and the City and Guilds London Institute.

Funding for further education prior to the Lauder Technical School came from a Local Taxation Act of 1890 which imposed additional duties on beer and spirits. After earmarking certain payments, it directed what was left to County Councils for, amongst other things, the purpose of Technical Education. To the credit of Fife they applied the whole grant for that purpose and within weeks of the passing of the Act, arrangements had been made for providing instruction in such subjects as agriculture, dairying, mining, cookery and navigation. It became a matter of strong debate that the progress of such education should be dependent upon the sale of beer and spirits (Whisky Tax).

Although the Lauder Technical School had not been officially opened until 10th October 1899, it had been operating part-time evening classes in weaving from Wednesday 20th September of that year. Mr Thomas Ferguson, from the Technical Institute Dundee, had been the first appointed teacher for weaving, one night a week at the remuneration of £1 per week during the term, along with travelling expenses.

Magnetism and electricity classes each Tuesday evening began on 26th September. Chemistry and Laboratory ran each Thursday evening from 28th September and Laboratory Work. Carpentry and Joinery in conjunction with Building Construction was offered every Wednesday evening from 7.00 pm until 9.00 pm from 27th September in accordance with the syllabus of the City and Guilds of London Institute. Mining Classes were held on Tuesday and Friday evenings, to help supply the 3,203 coalmines which were in operation with good quality mine managers. The first of these classes began on Tuesday 3rd October. The teacher was a Mr John Clarke, a Colliery Manager from the Rosebank Colliery.

The fee for each class was five shillings (twenty-five pence) or just seven shillings if two subjects were taken. However, many local employers were giving every encouragement to their employees to attend the new Technical School including the offer to repay the fees of those who joined the classes in return for a guaranteed number of attendances.

The reform of the school system under the Education Act of 1872 had made school attendance compulsory from age five to thirteen (raised to fourteen in 1883). This ensured a ready supply of young pupils for the Lauder Technical School from the High School, even with numerous exemptions and provision for "half-timers" (half day at school and half day at work).

Lauder Technical School worked very closely, as it had been intended to do, with its near neighbour, the old Dunfermline High School, and would operate, very often as a single unit. A pupil of the High School might pass from the one building to the other several times in the course of a day. The classes were kept working in unison by means of an electric clock which rang two bells in each building simultaneously to signal the start and finish of every school period and interval. This bell never rang on a Saturday or a Sunday nor did it ring between the hours of 4.00 pm and 9.00 am the following day.

The value of the two schools was not confined to the use that was made of them during the day by High School pupils. They were also a centre of educational activity in the evening with several hundred pupils, mainly young men but also some women, attending classes nightly, often following a very hard day at work at the mill or down the coal pits. It was not uncommon for some of the pupils to fall asleep during class through sheer exhaustion.

Prizes were offered to the best pupil of design, machine drawing and weaving construction. Mr William Mungall of the School Board agreed to provide a silver medal to the student who secured the highest marks in the class for weaving, an indication of the high demand for good skilled weavers at that time.

On the resignation of Mr George Dunn, the High School Rector, on 5th December 1898, the appointment of Dr Andrew Thomson became a non-starter as he declined the post before taking it up. Dr John MacDonald, Mathematics and Science Master in George Watson's College Edinburgh, was thus given the joint appointment as Rector of the High School and first new Rector of Lauder Technical School at a salary of £400 per annum by the School Board. Under Dr MacDonald's Rectorship the new Lauder School became an integral part of the community and flourished in its own right.

The early years of the Lauder Technical School were overshadowed by two events which were memorable for the saddest of reasons.

On 28th August 1901 an inrush of moss at the Donibristle Colliery killed eight miners, including four rescuers, who had gone down to search for their comrades and had also become trapped by further falls of moss. Heart-rending final messages of love to parents, wives, children and sweethearts were left from the dying miners written in chalk on the back of their shovels as time eventually ran out to save their lives. More than three months later, on Saturday 14th December, news came through that they had eventually found the bodies of the entombed miners at the Donibristle Colliery. On that very same day Fife was to lose one of its foremost thinkers and educationalists, the man whose name the new Technical School was proud to bear. Mr George Lauder had died on Saturday December 14th 1901, two years after the realisation of his educational dream. He was 87 years of age.

While the death of the miners was yet another reminder, if one was needed, of the true cost of coal, the death of George Lauder marked the end of one era and the beginning of another.

As the news of Lauder's death reached Andrew Carnegie, he recorded his feelings on a letter he received from uncle Lauder a few weeks previous:

*"The last note received from the man to whom I owe the most, and who was nearest and dearest to me of all men. My uncle and father, for such he was since I reached manhood."*

In another letter to his friend John Morely Carnegie wrote:

*"I feel so lonely, the intense interest he took in all my doings gave me satisfaction. How this will please Uncle Lauder! was always present in my mind as events came."*

George Lauder was dead but his legacy was only beginning. His reputation had gone far beyond the boundaries of Fife. His hard work and vision for education would ensure that through Lauder Technical School his spirit and sound principles would live on.

# The Lauder Bursary

Fife culture, dominated for so long by poverty and fear - fear of hunger, fear of the poorhouse and fear of unemployment, was the driving force behind the characteristically Scottish urge to 'get ahead and do well' but this was not always open to those who were in most need of the further education.

George Lauder's dream of free technical education for all had only been partially realised due to the many classes which could not be offered on a free basis. Even with the generous encouragement by local employers of their employees, those unemployed or with unsympathetic bosses could not take advantage of the new Lauder Technical School and were therefore at a disadvantage.

The Carnegie Dunfermline Trust Scholarship in 1903, under the Secretary W George MA, provided bursaries of up to £65 held for one or two years to enable promising weaving pupils to proceed to a University or Technical College or School of Art. Radical for its time. Special attention was given to claims from young women. This award was often mistakenly called the Lauder Bursary because of the many Lauder students who gained the award.

A limited number of free scholarships and bursaries were available, but only from primary schools to secondary schools, after 1906. Before this date many young pupils had to rely on precious few privately donated bursaries to see them through their education.

George Lauder Junior, of Pittsburgh America, cousin, friend and partner of Andrew Carnegie, left £1,700 in the year 1900 to provide a bursary in connection with the Lauder Technical School, to be open to competition by young men who had been engaged for at least three years in a mechanical or engineering subject, to encourage them to attend classes in the University of Glasgow or Edinburgh in that field.

George Lauder Junior himself had studied engineering at Glasgow University in 1860 before going to America to make his fortune alongside his cousin

Andrew Carnegie, and wished to help deserving students at the Lauder Technical School to take a course of engineering at University.

The Fund was known as the Lauder Bursary Fund and the rules and regulations governing the competition were drawn up by the School Board on 26th February 1900 in consultation with George Lauder Senior.

In later years the Fife Education Authority would award the bursary to the most meritorious candidate after such examination as they thought fit. According to a Minute of the first Electoral Area Committee of Fife Education Authority, 12th May 1925 the bursary was given on the following basis:

That the Lauder Bursary shall be £80 per annum for a period of three years, to be awarded triennially;

That the award be given to the student who takes first place in the engineering classes at Lauder Technical School. The head teacher of the school would give the names of those students eligible for consideration to the Electoral Area Committee together with a note of the marks gained by each in general class work and class examinations;

That the student should be at least three years in a mechanical occupation and qualified for admission to a University or reported as likely to secure such a qualification within a reasonable period;

That the successful student undertake to enter upon a course at either Glasgow University or Edinburgh University, leading to the award of the degree BSc in Engineering;

That the Bursary may be at any time withdrawn in the event of the receipt of an
unsatisfactory report as to attendance, conduct, or progress at the University;

That the Education Authority shall be sole judges for the qualification of an award of a Bursary or for the continuance of an award previously made.

Lauder Technical School was affiliated to the Heriot-Watt College and the

College of Art, Edinburgh. Students who attended courses at Lauder for four years were also eligible for the Senior Scholarship awarded by the Fife County Committee on Secondary Education for attendance at these Colleges during the day or evening.

Numerous students who were in receipt of the Lauder Bursary in turn became quite notable, particularly Alexander Cooper (1900 - 1903) who had the honour of being the first ever winner of a Lauder Bursary. Alex Ritchie, second winner of the award in 1903, went on to gain a Bachelor of Science in Engineering at Glasgow University, with distinction in Mathematics. Ritchie retired after 35 years service as Headmaster of Chatham Royal Dockyard School, a school which held the distinction of being the oldest Technical School in the world. Ritchie was awarded an MBE in 1944.

James Wilson (1906 - 1909), who gained degrees of BSc in Engineering and Mining, won ten class medals in the course of his BSc studies including King's prize for Mining 1902, King's prize for Applied Mechanics in 1903, the King's medal for Mining and the City and Guilds Medal in Mining Honours, Grade Three, 1905. This City and Guilds medal was reputed to be the first medal ever to be awarded north of the border.

Wilson was awarded a £60 bursary in two cheque instalments, £40 for the winter term and £20 for the summer term. While Wilson was a student at Glasgow he helped with classes at Cowdenbeath and also taught evening classes in Mining at the Lauder Technical School in 1910. He then travelled to India where he spent 27 years as Mining Engineer and Superintendent with the Indian Railway.

In his memoirs, James was to write of his fond memories at the Lauder Technical School:

*"It is a long time since I left what was then known as the Lauder Technical School, but I have happy and grateful memories of the enjoyable and profitable years of study there. Who couldn't with such admirable, kindly and efficient teachers. Doing my best in order to be a credit to the old school, I gained many prizes at Glasgow University and was awarded the degrees of B.Sc in Engineering and Mining, with special distinction in engineering drawing, geology and mineralogy - my favourite subjects. On the whole I have had a good time and it has all been due to the help given me by the Lauder Technical School."*

Mr Stewart Anderson, another of the Lauder Bursary winners, wrote from Toronto in Canada:

*"My most vivid memories of the Lauder Technical School was the devoted interest in the majority of the lads, many of whom had truly remarkable attendance records, despite shift work, etc. I particularly admired the three boys who made the journey three times every week, from Perth."*

John M Lessells, who was a student and prizewinner in 1910, went on to become editor of the international publication 'Journal of Applied Mechanics' for over thirty years. In 1936 he became a professor of Mechanical Engineering at the Massachusetts Institute of Technology and helped design the mounting for the 200" telescope on Mount Palomar in California. Mr Lessells was also an author of several publications on Engineering which were transferred into several different languages.

Lessells was to write:

*"I owe a great deal to the inspiration I received in my early years in Dunfermline with the Lauder Technical School."*

John Lessells died in May 1961 while engaged in his final project, "Reminiscences of a Former Lauder Scholar."

James Walton who emigrated to Concord, North Carolina, USA was top student in the weaving class in 1906 and was awarded the Carnegie Trust Scholarship to the value of £80 along with the William Mungall medal. He later chose to go to Manchester Technical College. Out of all of the students in Great Britain, Walton came top in the City and Guilds examination, honours section, for linen weaving. Along with the first class certificate he was also awarded a Gold Medal and three pounds. He also received the first class certificate and Gold Medal for jute weaving.

*"I would not have been able to take some of the positions I have had in America, if it had not been for the valuable teaching I got at the Lauder Technical School"* wrote Mr Walton in 1961. When Mr Walton died in May 1967 the North Carolina's 'News and Observer' described him as the oldest living graduate of Lauder Technical Institute, Scotland.

During the term 1923-27 James Rae was a Diploma student in the Textile Class and later on the teaching staff of Lauder Technical School. He wrote from South Africa in 1961 with a great sense of "gratification" when he recalled the names of G (Dod) Izatt, R Hay and G McGregor, A R Geary, Headmaster, co-teachers H Cook and A M Reekie and R (Bob) Thomson and a special tribute to the late Thomas Milne.

*"The Lauder "Tech" has always offered satisfactory methods for training and educating young persons"* wrote Mr Rae, *"and so the opportunity is presented for men and women who intend to succeed. The real significance of good, general education is being realised today and I should like to see the "Old School" be given a higher status in the future, nearer to University level.*

*I repeat this note in Afrikaans, our other official language, in order to stress the fact that linguistic barriers are a greater impediment to easy international acceptance than most students of technology realise."*

After 1892 bursaries for those who could not afford to pursue further education became more widely available in those secondary and technical schools where fees had not been abolished. However, these bursaries continued to be meritocratic rather than democratic and reflected the main ethos of the Scottish education system itself. Students were selected by competitive examination and needed to have previously attended for three years at a state-aided school and required to demonstrate that they had a clear aim to follow a full curriculum of secondary education. Bursaries could be withdrawn for a number of reasons, including bad attendance or failure to make the stated grade. In one example in the School Minute of 1909, a bursary granted to Edward Barrie had been withdrawn because he had also gained a "Berry Bursary."

Owing to the First World War, the Carnegie Trust Scholarships were suspended after 1914 whereafter the development of the Education Scotland Act caused the trustees to decide to discontinue it altogether.

However in 1927 the scholarship was revived when the Education Authority approached the Trust with a request to contribute to the maintenance and expenses of students seeking courses which could not be provided by Scottish central institutions. The scholarship was £120 and would normally be held for three years. For the period 1927 to 1930 the scholarship was awarded to James Rae but only after one Henry Cook had enigmatically declined to accept the offer.

The Lauder Bursary remained in operation until 1958 when it was amalgamated with the Fife Educational Trust.

## Lauder Bursars 1900 - 1935

| Year | Name |
| --- | --- |
| 1900-1903 | Cooper Alexander |
| 1903-1906 | Ritchie Alex |
| 1906-1909 | Wilson James |
| 1909-1912 | Weir David |
| 1912-1914 | Lessells John M |
| 1914- | George Hoggan |
| 1919-1923 | Spittal James |
| 1924- | McKinlay Alex |
| 1931-1932 | Thomson Robert |
| 1932-1935 | Lunan John |
| 1936-1939 | Walker Thomas M |

## Carnegie Trust Bursars 1904 - 1935

| Year | Name |
| --- | --- |
| 1904-1905 | Beveridge James P |
| 1905-1906 | Henderson Laurie |
| 1906-1908 | Walton James |
| 1908 1910 | Murray Ebenezer |
| 1910-1911 | Smeaton James |
| 1913-1914 | Shearer Ronald G |
| 1927-1930 | Rae James |
| 1930-1935 | Kilgour Ronald M |

In 1990 the Carnegie Dunfermline Trust kindly provided the College with £500 per annum for 5 years to allow building students to travel and view foreign developments.

FIFE EDUCATION AUTHORITY.

*Lauder Technical School* Continuation Classes.

*Linen Weaving* Course.

Year *III*

This is to Certify that

*James Rae*

has attended the above Course of Instruction under Division *III* of the Code of Regulations for Continuation Classes during Session *1925-6*, and that *he* was awarded the following Marks for Diligence and Progress:—

*Linen Weaving* 76 ¼ %    Hours of Attendance *140* out of *144*.
*Chemistry*      70 %

G. *MacGregor*

*Director of Education.*

*First* CLASS CERTIFICATE.

Lauder Technical School Continuation Classes.
This First Class Certificate was awarded to James Rae for Linen Weaving in 1926.

Winners of the Miss Elizabeth S. Lauder Swimming Trophy at the Carnegie Baths 1910 beside their headmaster Dr John MacDonald seated centre. Miss Lauder presented the trophy to the Carnegie Dunfermline Trustees for boys and girls of the public schools of Dunfermline in 1910 to provide swimming and life-saving trophies for boys and girls under 15 years of age. Alongside the Lauder Bursary this was another example of the Lauder influence in all matters educational (which would have a practical influence on the youth of Fife). (DPL LHC)

James Wilson became the third person in Lauder history to win a Lauder Bursary. He gained degrees of BSc in Engineering and Mining and won ten class medals in the course of his BSc studies. Wilson taught for Lauder Technical School in 1910 while still a student at Glasgow. He travelled to India where he spent 27 years as Mining Engineer and Superintendent with the Indian Railway.

John M Lessels, a Lauder student and prize winner in 1910, went on to become editor of the International publication 'Journal of Applied Mechanics' for over 30 years. In 1936 he became a professor of Mechanical Engineering of the Massachusetts Institute of Technology. "I owe a great deal to the inspiration I received in my early years in Dunfermline with the Lauder Technical School."

James Walton was top student in the weaving class of 1906 and was awarded the 'Carnegie Trust Scholarship' to the value of £80, along with the William Mungall medal. "I would not have been able to take some of the positions I have had in America, if it had not been for the valuable teaching I got at the Lauder Technical School" wrote Mr Walton in 1961.

Ebenezer L Murray who gained the Carnegie Trust Scholarship the year after James Walton.

# The "Red-Tech" Extension

The reputation of the Lauder School had, like its founder, spread so far and wide that it was not long before it was operating to its full capacity with people travelling from all over Fife and beyond to receive first class technical education.

Lauder Technical School possessed such up to date equipment, including a good supply of meteorological instruments which were used to give weekly and monthly reports to the local newspapers and the Scottish Meteorological Society, that they were the envy of many Scottish Schools and Colleges at that time.

Along with the excellent equipment there was also a provision for special teachers of Building Construction, Architecture, Design and Advanced Art to be brought in from Edinburgh and Glasgow. In this way some of the most progressive educational minds in the country were placed within the reach of the Lauder students. This ensured that Lauder had the happy problem of very well attended evening classes which were highly popular.

Up until the building of the Lauder Technical School, little had been done to provide properly equipped classrooms suitable for the instruction of adults. This became another first for the Technical School which was to prove its value over the numerous decades.

The old High School was said to have been fairly well suited to theoretical work alongside its new Lauder neighbour which, although well equipped for vocational education, was nevertheless like the old High School, straining under the sheer volume it was having to deal with in the early years of its existence. Of the 839 students enrolled for the term 1906 in connection with the various evening schools around Dunfermline, 340 of them were attending the Lauder Technical School alone. Of the 46 teachers employed, 23 were on the Lauder School staff.

In an 'Educational Institute of Scotland' Congress Handbook in January 1906, the following statement was made with regard to the new Lauder Technical School:

*"If any visitors desire to see the best of our schools they may visit the Lauder Technical School which we consider a splendid building. It is only a few years since it was erected and it was supposed to be large enough for the wants of many years, but it is now taxed beyond its accommodation, and this school and its ally and neighbour the High School both urgently demand great extensions and must form a troublesome problem for the next School Board."*

In 1907 Carnegie was furious when Dr John Ross, Chairman of the Carnegie Trust, put forward plans for a separate textile school. He scorned Ross's idea and offered funding for a new Lauder extension to accommodate, among other things, the demands for weaving.

Industries all over Scotland had been increasing output in spectacular fashion in the period between 1870 and 1914 - steel, shipbuilding, coal, heavy engineering and construction. By 1910, a welcome increase of activity in the linen trade was experienced, with the manufacturers going from short time working to overtime working in a short period of time. It meant, as George Lauder had predicted, that there was an even greater demand for technical education than ever before and this was reflected in the rising demand for places at the Lauder Technical School.

It came as no surprise to anyone that proposals for a structural extension to Lauder School building were put forward by the Burgh School Board as early as January 1902. However, it was not until a special meeting of the Board in January 1909 that any serious consideration of an extension to the Lauder Technical School was given following further funds being made available from their old friend Andrew Carnegie.

*"If justice was to be done to several of the subjects taught there, (Lauder Technical School) especially those of weaving, engineering and mining, a large addition to the present building must be faced,"* said the School Board. *"Even under the cramped conditions which prevailed excellent work was being done and now an opportunity had arisen which if proved successful should secure to Dunfermline for many years to come the premier place in Fife for technical and secondary education."*

With only one dissenting voice the Board was in full agreement to the need for larger premises for the Lauder Technical School. The further decision of whether to add an extension to the present building or whether to erect a new building altogether was now the point of consideration. However, the conditions in which Andrew Carnegie had made a further offer of funding available was on the basis that a new building be erected.

The new Lauder extension was built of red Dunfermline sandstone. It was nicknamed 'The Red-Tech' as opposed to the 'Grey Tech', which was the original Lauder Technical School. It was twelve feet back from the pavement in New Row and consisted of three stories with attics, eighty-two feet in length and forty-eight feet in width. Both the 'Red Tech' and the 'Grey Tech' were of such architectural merit that they became listed buildings. To the rear of this central block was a weaving shed and a boiler house. Cloakrooms, lavatories and cellar accommodation were in the basement. The ground floor held accommodation for a mechanical laboratory, a heat laboratory, a department for textile design and analysis and a weaving lecture room. The upper floor was devoted to machine drawing, a lecture room, a chemical laboratory and an electrical laboratory. Accommodation for the teachers was provided in the attic flat.

The new extension, not quite completed, was officially opened on the evening of Thursday 13th October 1910 by Lord Shaw, when a large number of invited guests assembled in the High School gymnasium for the ceremony. On the platform that day was Rev John Sanderson, Chairman of the School Board, presiding. Supporting him on the platform were Lord Shaw, Mr J C Smith, HM Inspector of schools for Fife, Dr Ross, Mr C D Allister and Mr James Mitchell, organising secretary for the Secondary Education Committee of the Fife County Council, and others.

The Chairman opened with the words:

*" . . .Great doubts and fears were freely expressed that the building that was opened some eleven years ago was likely, on account of its great size to prove a "white elephant" to the community. However, before long those doubts and fears had been falsified with the new increased accommodation which soon became necessary. From that small beginning that was made in those early days of 1899 they had now some 400 students attending Technical classes in Dunfermline."*

The extension had been made possible from two directions. A grant of £5,300 from the Scotch Education Department, and from Mr Carnegie a further gift of £3,300. In round figures the total cost of the building was £11,000 of which only £3,400 was required from the local authorities.

Lord Shaw spoke of the gospel of technical education and the need for such education, like that given in the Lauder Technical School, to be developed all over the country:

*"At one time technical education was often seen as something that was far above the ordinary working man. This had to be overcome to show that this was not the case and that technical education was simply a co-operation of nature with brain.*

*Technical education, relative to secondary education is a most costly affair... That is the reason why technical education may have lingered a little on its road in Scotland because it has been allied with a need for heavy expense."*

Following the speeches a key of solid silver and gold gilt was presented to Lord Shaw by the Chairman of the School Board. On one side of the key was the words *"Burgh School Board, Addition to Lauder Technical School"* and on the other side the words *"Presented to Lord Shaw of Dunfermline."*

On the conclusion of the speeches the party walked round to New Row where they surrounded the steps of the school. Lord Shaw, having opened the door, said:

*"Ladies and Gentlemen I have now with the beautiful gift that you have been kind enough to present to me opened the door of the new building.*

*I beg to declare now, so long as stone and lime shall last and education beloved in this district, men women and children shall know and feel the benefits of it, so long will this building be open for all students to receive its instruction. May you be guided by wisdom and counsel higher than your own in order to utilise all the capacities of your citizens for the higher good of your generation and country."*

The gathered assembly then went inside 'The Red-Tech' for a privileged view of the various departments of the new Lauder extension.

The Red Tech (the new Lauder extension) was built in 1910 as a result of increased demand by industry for technical education as predicted by George Lauder. The Wilson Institute to the right of the new Lauder extension was another of the many annexes which Lauder made use of. (DPL LHC)

Provost John Allan whose name was closely linked with Lauder College over many years.

The Allan Institute of Lauder Technical School was named after Mr Allan.

Apprentices busy at work at Lauder's Machine Shop at the old 'Red-Tech' which opened on 13 October 1910. Their skills were in great demand.

# Fife Mining School

As Lauder Technical School expanded and developed its facilities to cater for ever increasing demand, one important feature of its development was the merger with the Fife Mining School at Cowdenbeath.

The Fife Mining School was founded in 1890 by Andrew S Cunningham, editor of The Dunfermline and West Fife Journal (now defunct), and was the first of its kind in the east of Scotland. Prior to this date, several unsuccessful attempts had been made in various parts of Fife to establish evening classes in Mining and Engineering.

Cunningham had written a series of articles in his newspaper in 1889 backing such campaigners as George Lauder in the need for Technical Education in Fife and had suggested that special attention be given to Mining and Agriculture. Later he called a meeting of the Coal Owners, Miners Leaders and others interested in education at which it was decided to found the Fife Mining School with Cunningham as its Secretary.

At its inaugural meeting in the old High School, Dunfermline in 1890 over 80 students enrolled and a Mr Williamson was appointed Mining Lecturer and part-time Principal on a salary of £50. He also taught classes at Hamilton. Classes were entirely confined to the evenings and students were trained for the Science and Art examination and Colliery Managers' Certificate. The course fee for Mining and Mechanics was fifteen shillings and sixpence per session (seventy-seven and a half pence). Cunningham obtained travelling concessions from the Railway Company to help these students, many of whom had to travel long distances by rail, bicycle and shoe-leather, to attend the school.

The school, established as a private enterprise, was supported by the Coal Owners, with accommodation and equipment being provided by the Dunfermline School Board. Grants based on examination results together with the "Whisky Tax" allocation also helped to support the school in its early years. Subjected to all the inconveniences and uncertainties which flow from a small and irregular income, the school was soon in financial trouble. There were also doubts as to whether in fact it was eligible for 'Whisky Tax' money since the school was not under the control of the Local Authority.

A new branch of the Mining School was opened in 1892 but Cunningham was not satisfied that the school could go on as it had been doing, the premises being poor and inadequate. However, even with these difficulties he still wanted to extend and expand the school and its work. Using his newspaper for this purpose he suggested that the Dunfermline School Board should take over the Mining School and that they should either build a new school or purchase the Wilson School in Dunfermline at an estimated cost of £1,000. He further suggested that the pernicious system of payment by results be abolished and that teachers be placed on a yearly salary basis.

By 1893 a small anti-technical school committee had been formed and using terms like "supreme folly" and "gross extravagance" drew up a petition to oppose the provision of a technical school which it was estimated almost 80% of the voters in Dunfermline signed. On the presentation of this petition the School Board resigned as a body, regarding the petition as a vote of no confidence. This in effect left Dunfermline without a School Board for several months.

In 1895, as a result of difficulties, the Fife Mining School transferred to larger premises in Cowdenbeath where mining was predominant and simultaneously Cunningham agreed to hand over control to the County Technical Education Committee. By the year 1897 Mr Williamson's salary had gone up to £70 plus half the Science and Art grant plus £10 travelling expenses. The transference of the Mining School to Cowdenbeath in 1895 left Dunfermline without any form of technical training until the opening of the Lauder Technical School in 1899.

In 1901, Hamilton Academy claimed Mr Williamson's undivided service, and Mr Joseph Parker, ex-Colliery Manager at Bowhill Colliery and Mining Lecturer in Fife from 1894, was appointed to succeed him. Dr Parker's subject was Mine Ventilation for which he gained the award of Doctor of Science from the University of Edinburgh. Dr Parker was also part-time lecturer in Mining at the Heriot-Watt College from 1902-1907. The success of the School was maintained under Parker and the curriculum became broader and more systematic, but there was still a need for increased facilities.

A report by HM Inspector of Schools in 1906 recommended additional laboratory space where students could carry out practical work in mechanics, chemistry and electrical engineering. Later in 1906 it was agreed by the Technical Committee that new premises were required. The problem for the Committee was whether to build the new premises in Cowdenbeath or Dunfermline. A conference was arranged to discuss the position with representatives from Dunfermline School Board, Beath School Board, Coal Owners, Miners Union, the County Council and Scottish Education Department in attendance. At this meeting it was shown that most of the students came from the Cowdenbeath area. The Beath School Board agreed to provide several rooms for the accommodation of a Mining School in the buildings of a new Higher Grade School which was being erected on condition that the Beath School Board be financially compensated.

An aerial view of Cowdenbeath Technical College. Originally founded in 1890 it was called the Fife Mining School. It transferred its premises from Dunfermline to Cowdenbeath in 1895. In 1952 it changed its name to Cowdenbeath Technical College. A round of pit closures in the 1960s seriously affected the College and it was amalgamated with Lauder in 1967 under the one name of Lauder Technical College.

Prior to the opening of the Mining School, the Burgh of Cowdenbeath was experiencing a severe recession in its development. Mining, on which its population was mainly dependent for its livelihood, had been in trouble. The first serious trial was that connected with the struggle over the maintenance of the minimum standard wage of six shillings per day. Even though full time was the exception rather than the rule and trade was at a low ebb there was still a feeling of optimism, of better times ahead.

The total expenditure for the Mining School was in the region of £3,000 with local subscriptions coming from: Coal Owners £1,000, Scottish Education Department, £1,000 and Fife County Council £800.

The new Fife Mining School at Stenhouse Street was opened in September 1910 and for the first time it was made possible for students to take a three year course in Mining in either morning or evening classes, although the vast majority still attended evening classes. From 1909 up to 1939 the staff of the school consisted of the Principal, three full-time and forty part-time teachers, the work still being mostly confined to evenings.

When the 1914-1918 war started, many of the Mining School students enlisted in August and September of that year. Many more came to the school office to enquire whether they could enlist or enrol and whether it would be possible for the school to give military training in addition to their ordinary courses of study. This request was sanctioned by the School Committee on condition that those receiving such military training should agree to join the colours at the end of their training. In October 1914 the Fife Mining School Corps (voluntary) was formed and affiliated to the Mechanical Transport Army Service Corps.

Two hundred students enrolled and the training included Physical Exercise, Military Drill, instruction on the petrol engine and motor car driving. Later, full-time practical training was given in the turning and screwcutting of munitions which continued to the end of the War. In May 1915 the first batch of 150 students enlisted for War Service from the Fife Mining School.

In 1920 Dr Parker went to great lengths to change the name of the Fife Mining School to include the words "and Engineering College" but without success.

After the war the Mining School continued to expand which led to a shortage of accommodation. In 1930 the Higher Education Committee agreed that accommodation was inadequate and recommended that suitable extra accommodation should be erected in the school playground. In December 1930 the Miners' Welfare Commission allocated £15,000 towards the new premises and the idea of building at Stenhouse Street was abandoned. Following several considerations for a new site, including a disused linen factory behind the railway station, the site at Broad Street was given preference and the new Fife Mining School was opened in 1936.

In 1922 the Institute of Mechanical Engineers suggested the introduction of National Certificated Courses in Technical Colleges. Dr Parker, the Principal of the Mining School, was an enthusiastic supporter of this scheme. He felt that the course had a definite objective and gave a very welcome stimulus to the efforts of the student. Fife Mining School was among the first in Scotland, certainly by several years the first in Fife, to adopt National Certificated Courses. In May 1931 the first (12) students were presented for the Ordinary National Certificate in Electrical Engineering.

In 1935 all boys entering the Mining industry in Fife were required to attend special 'Safety In Mines' classes. These classes met one evening a week over a term of twenty weeks with approximately 300 boys attending the course during the first year.

In 1936 a large Engineering Workshop was built on the east side of the main building. Dr Joseph Parker resigned in December 1936 and was succeeded by Mr R Nelson.

The first advanced part-time Mining day classes commenced in September 1938 and ten Mining students with good records of attendance and progress in evening classes over a period of five years were awarded Scholarships by the Miners' Welfare Commission. The Coal Companies had now agreed to release the students one day a week but not to pay for wages lost. However a grant of ten shillings a week to cover loss of wages was made by the Miners' Welfare Commission which eased the situation considerably for the students.

The increased number of machine tools and power units in the school required constant attention to keep them in working order. After numerous difficulties and objections a full time mechanic was finally appointed in 1939. During the 1939-1945 War the mechanic was absorbed into the teaching staff and helped with the instruction of soldiers.

During the Second World War the Mining School once again gave a special act of grace in the form of technical training for service personnel. The training of soldiers began in 1940 and continued until 1945 with approximately 750,000 student hours of instruction given to over 1,800 soldiers. Courses included Mining, Surveying, Fitting, Turning, Motor Vehicles, Wireless and Blacksmithing. The length of the courses varied from 4 to 16 weeks. One period classes were conducted on the shift system and the school session ran 24 hours a day. The special instruction to soldiers involved many full-time teacher appointments but the scheme was completely self-supporting. The training was carried out in addition to the day to day school work and equalled in volume 20 normal years.

In the early days of the War, the Mining School was expeditiously "blacked out" by the staff and was ready to commence work on the normal operating date. Although enrolments had dropped by 50% and attendances during the War period were at a very low ebb, there was still a slight increase in staff.

A Cinema Projectionist Class was started in September 1949 and became firmly established and, though numbers were small, students were drawn from all over Fife and attended one half day per week for a period of three years.

The advent of the National Coal Board led to an explosion in the student population and a more generous policy of day release for mine workers. Fife Mining School was approved for both HNC and ONC in Electrical and Mechanical Engineering on a day release and evening basis prior to 1950; together with MQB Mine Managers and Mine Surveyors qualifications on a Day Release and Evening basis. The first presentations at Ordinary National Certificate level were in 1952 and Higher National Certificate in 1954. Since the start of the scheme, 123 students gained Ordinary National Certificates and 58 gained Higher National Certificates. Further developments included HND Mining, HNC Mining, HNC Mining Surveying as well as a full range of

Ordinary National Certificate courses.

Following the appointment of William J Morris to Principal in 1957 the name of Fife Mining School changed to Cowdenbeath Technical College.

A round of pit closures in the 1960s began to affect student numbers and there was a major rationalisation of education provision in Fife. As a result William J Morris eventually went to Kirkcaldy Technical College in 1967.

The earlier connection between the town of Dunfermline and the old 'Fife Mining School' was re-established in 1967 when 'Lauder Technical College' and 'Cowdenbeath Technical College' were amalgamated under the one name, 'Lauder Technical College' and under one Principal, Stewart Liddle.

Lauder catered for all mining courses up to Ordinary National Certificate level as well as specialist mining courses. Lauder also ran specialist courses developed in conjunction with the National Coal Board to cater for advances in new technology and students from Lothian, Central and Strathclyde regions attended. Following a successful pilot stage these courses were turned over to City and Guilds London Institute for registration and certification.

This helped to stabilise total student numbers at around 350 per year in a wide variety of traditional and specialist fields. In addition, Lauder was the only College in Fife approved by the MQB to conduct the statutory Gas Testing and Heating Examinations which deputies and shotfirers had to undertake and pass every five years.

A moratorium on the recruitment of electrical and mechanical apprentices in 1980, and the aftermath of the miners strike in 1984/5 reduced student numbers to such a level that, after consultation with British Coal, it was decided to run-down the Mining Departments of Colleges in Scotland. Lauder and Kirkcaldy were the last two to survive in Scotland. Courses were completed in 1990 thus ending 100 years of mining education in Fife.

A group of secretarial girls outside the Cowdenbeath Technical College in 1965. A uniform was very much a part of daily life for the student then, as well as a beehive hairstyle!

# Lauder Technical School: 1910-1945

Following the opening of Lauder's 'Red-Tech' extension in 1910 the Textile School, as it also came to be known, continued to develop and prosper. New classes were formed, additional teachers were appointed and there was a great increase in the number of students. One such new appointment for Lauder was that of Mr Thomas Milne, Weaving Master, who had come from Dundee Technical College to Dunfermline in 1901. Following the building of the 'Red Tech' extension in New Row the School Board were keen to extend their field of operations to include the craft of weaving. Mr Milne superintended the installation of the looms and other appliances in the school and soon had a full evening class of enthusiastic students drawn from all the linen factories in Dunfermline. In addition to writing many informative and interesting articles for technical journals, Milne was the joint author of two books entitled "Jute and Linen Weaving" and "Textile Design, Pure and Applied" both of which were recognised as standard works in their field.

In addition to the subjects which were already being taught, namely Art and Design, Engineering and Building Construction, there were added Weaving, Mining, Chemistry, Electricity, Commercial Training and Carpentry. From time to time other subjects were added such as Plumbing, House-Painting and Tailoring. In subjects such as Design and Architecture more advanced classes were formed and taught by specially qualified visiting masters from Edinburgh and Glasgow.

The Science and Art classes, which had originally been taught in an old church hall in1881 by the Headmaster of Lauder Technical School, Mr John Robertson, were taken over by the Education Department and treated as part of the Evening Continuation School system. This was followed by efforts to co-ordinate and systematise the work of the Evening Schools in general, to raise the standards of education, and to induce students to follow graded courses of study extending over a number of sessions. These efforts were largely successful with the character and quality of the work becoming more advanced.

However, by early 1914 storm clouds were gathering with the prospect of a

World War. Andrew Carnegie, who had sold up his vast empire of steel in 1902, found a new mission in life which reflected his late Uncle Lauder's philosophy of pacifism. The radical nature of Lauder's political beliefs, in sharp contrast with the mildness of his character, disposed Lauder to impress into Carnegie's mind a hatred of war and military display which stayed with him throughout his life. Carnegie, who had by then rediscovered his radical roots, had a vision whereby he, Theodore Roosevelt of America and Kaiser Wilhelm of Germany would meet together and discuss his programme for a new 'Peace of Nations'. The President and the Kaiser would enthusiastically accept this vision thus putting an end to any thoughts of war. Of the two leaders, Carnegie regarded the Kaiser as being the more important and the more certain of fulfilling his vision for peace. Carnegie worked tirelessly for peace and met with Kaiser Wilhelm in 1913 when he congratulated him on his peaceful twenty-five year reign before discussing the possibility of some kind of 'Peace of Nations' treaty, but it came to nothing.

Carnegie, still believing he was able to influence war events for the good, refused to give up his battle to win peace and wrote Kaiser Wilhelm a letter in October 1914 suggesting that he accept a proposed peace treaty of giving statesmen a year to cool, which he hoped would be sufficient time to ensure peace upon some kind of terms. The Kaiser agreed to Carnegie's proposal but, following the sinking of the cruise ship Lusitania in the spring of 1915, it was too late to have any hope of ratification or peace.

Carnegie celebrated his 83rd birthday, two weeks after the end of the War in November 1918. It was his last. He died in Lenox, Massachusetts on 11th August 1919.

It is impossible to underestimate the influence of a world war on educational thinking and society in general. Many Lauder students, like Ronald G Shearer, broke off their studies to join the call to arms from the Prime Minister Herbert Asquith who was promising that "they would be treated as never before." The King's shilling was no substitute for a Lauder Bursary. James Spittle, on deciding to join the colours and in receipt of one such Bursary in early 1914, wrote to the Fife Education Authorities to make sure that he would be able to continue with his studies and his bursary where he left off following cessation of hostilities. They informed him that, victory assured, this would be honoured.

Spittle not only survived the war but returned to his studies in 1919 graduating BSc in Mechanical Engineering at Glasgow University in 1923.

As a result of the many students who enlisted for war duties, the numbers of Lauder School attendees dropped significantly. Labour scarcity in general and great shortages of basic foods like eggs, milk, meat and potatoes made price controls and rationing a fact of daily life. Coal output grew because of its relationship to other heavy industries but partly also because foreign demand for coal in the run up to and beyond the War was buoyant. Great shortages apart, the variety of occupations which carried on within Fife connected with agriculture, weaving, engineering and mining, prevented the predominance of any one type of course at the Lauder Technical School and created in the mind of the student a readiness to receive new ideas, to test new methods, and a general adaptability.

Smoke of industry proved a more potent force than the smoke of artillery following the end of the War. However, many of those young lads who had joined up found the battle to secure any kind of employment equally difficult. A Lock-Out of miners by the Coal Owners in 1921 resulted in closure of all pits and mines and caused a storm of feeling in many of the Fife towns. In the mining town of Cowdenbeath, for example, batons and stones were used in a series of clashes between police and miners. This had limited effect on classes at Lauder which still continued to be popular.

Following the death of Mr Thomas Milne in 1922, assistant Mr Robert Thomson, who was also the Textile School janitor, took over the role of Weaving Teacher until such time as a replacement for Mr Milne could be found. It was not long before one such teacher was found in the shape of Mr Andrew Geary from the north of Ireland who took over the role as Weaving Instructor in the Textile School in late 1922. In a report submitted by Geary to the Fife Education Authority in 1923, he put forward a suggestion of having an assistant teacher, or tenter, in order to be able to "impart adequate practical instruction" to the growing number of students.

A week later the temporary appointment of Mr Robert Thomson, janitor of the Textile School, as mechanical assistant to Mr Geary took place. Thomson was to get an extra payment of ten shillings (fifty pence) per week and Geary was to get his assistant. In that same year of 1923, Andrew Geary was appointed Headmaster of the Textile School, taking over from the previous Headmaster Mr Anderson.

In 1927 eminent scientist Dr Haldane declared that *"The inhalation of coal dust causes no danger to life, but on the contrary gives protection against the development of tuberculosis"*. In that same year the Textile School was merged with the Lauder Technical School and Mr Andrew Geary became Headmaster of the combined 'Lauder' operation, a post he held for 28 years.

One piece of news with a Lauder connection which made international headlines in October 1928 was the marriage of the former world boxing heavy-weight champion and legend Gene Tunney to Miss Josephine Lauder, great grand-daughter of the other legend George Lauder. In a combined civil and religious ceremony in Italy, the two were married by the Fascist leader and lawyer, Signor Brofferio and by Monsignor Breslin.

Miss Lauder chose a man in whom there were many similarities to that of her own great grandfather. The son of a poor Irish immigrant, James Joseph Eugene Tunney's rise to public acclaim, like that of George Lauder, was a triumph of sacrifice, self-denial, and hard work. Tunney was a fighter who made a lightning raid on the boxing ring, made a fortune, and sensibly departed while still in condition to enjoy the fruits of his labour. Taking the title from Jack Dempsey, he held the crown from September 1926 to August 1928 when he retired from boxing, unbeaten at thirty years of age.

Like George Lauder, Tunney believed in the power of education and was one of the first boxers to use films of fights to observe the techniques of champions and opponents. He studied for the world title mentally and physically, as students would study for a degree. When he reached the top he had no intentions of staying long. *"Boxing,"* he informed the fight fraternity, *"has no attractive features for me. It is a brutal sport."*

Tunney was a true intellectual. He was a scholar and an authority on Shakespeare, a student of Kant and Spinoza, a friend of Somerset Maugham, Hugh Walpole, Thornton Wilder and George Bernard Shaw. After his retirement he won a prize in literature of £1,000, seeing off a professor along the way. He was the author of "A Man Must Fight", one of the few classics ever written on boxing literature. His literary tastes and habit of reading poetry, coupled with his refusal to send insulting messages to his opponents, did not make him a favourite with the sporting Press in America, but the news of his marriage to Miss Lauder made him a national hero in the United States. Like her great grandfather Miss Lauder was a keen student of literature and philosophy, and it was this similarity of tastes which first drew the two of them together and made for such a good match.

Technical education during the interwar years was in general very slow to develop while the economy suffered a reverse of good fortune that cut to the quick the self-confidence of the Scottish nation. The coalfields of Lanarkshire and Ayrshire were gradually contracting while those in Fife, much to the benefit of the Lauder classes, grew with great haste. The system of half-timers and exemptions at school operated with necessity and was not completely abolished until 1936. Only in 1945 was the general school-leaving age for all pupils raised to fifteen.

Change was coming from all directions and in 1929 Lauder Technical School was taken over by the Fife Education Authority. Many important decisions on subjects such as technical education were being taken quietly and in less public places than grand Acts of Parliament in the run up to and beyond World War Two. Change to the established view of education was coming from the mobilisation of ordinary people as represented by the rise of the Trades Unions, the Labour Party and the growing electoral power of the working class, which now included the voice of women. This in turn led to some of the greatest changes of all coming from the transformed personal and social expectations of ordinary people as they began to assert their new found influence.

Lauder's job now was to stay up to date and even ahead of those pioneers who were so often ahead of legislation. But then staying ahead was the very essence of the Lauder Legacy.

As if to confirm this the 'Spens Report' of 1938 advocated changes in education which were to bring in "a new type of higher school of a technical character," the type of school which Lauder had put into practice some forty years previous. Even so practical and technical education was still regarded as superfluous in most secondary and continuation classes, other than Lauder, until after the Second World War. In the same year as the 'Spens Report' at an annual presentation of certificates and prizes at Lauder Technical School, students and teachers were congratulated on achieving a record number of certificates gained in external examinations. Councillor George Izatt, Chairman of the Education Committee of Fife County Council, said:

*"I thought that Lauder had reached a maximum of success in external examinations two years ago, it was good even for their Chairman to be wrong."*

They had not reached their maximum then, and the figures that night proved that they had reached new heights, created new records, and so added to the great tradition of the Lauder Technical School.

To demonstrate Lauder's progress since 1932, Mr Izatt gave details as to the number of passes each year:

1932 - 32 passes, 1933 - 39 passes, 1934 - 50 passes, 1935 - 57 passes, 1936 - 71 passes, 1937 - 86 passes, 1938 - 90 passes.

Thanking those who took an interest in Lauder Technical School he said:

*"They had many employers, organisations of the workers, individual employers and quite a number of adults who came and supervised and took an interest in the various classes in the school. I do not think that we could find a closer co-operation between, teacher and student anywhere than in Lauder Technical School and without that, they could not have gained these excellent results."*

Dr William Reid of the Fife Coal Company Limited who presented the certificates and prizes said that the mining industry strongly believed in education. He went on to say that one of the worse things the mining industry had a reputation for was its accidents. Following a visit to America in 1934 they believed that these accidents could be reduced to a very large extent so they had decided on a programme of education to make certain that their officials and men realised the dangers and the best ways of reducing these accidents. By 1938, as a result of this education, accident rates had halved. *"I am pleased to say that for the first eight months of this year, we had only four fatalities as against eight during the first eight months of the previous year; there was thus a 50% reduction in fatalities".*

Dr Reid said he wanted them to realise that the man who was employed in the mining industry was very essential, not only to the community, but to the country. In other industries the mining man was rather looked down upon. He wanted them to get away from that idea, because if they met him as he had met him, they would find that the miner was a "real fellow" and he was doing his bit to keep them going as well.

Congratulating those who were receiving prizes and certificates that night for the first time, Dr Reid said that the men and women in this country who were most fitted for leadership were those who had broadened their minds and augmented their practical experience by study. He hoped that those who had completed their courses would continue their studies in everyday life. The Lauder Technical School had done great work in the past and had provided the basis for many successful careers. The success of the School was in part due to the teachers and to Mr Geary, the Headmaster, but to a greater extent to the students themselves.

On 28th October 1939 an explosion occurred at the Fife Coal Company, Valleyfield Colliery, as a result of firedamp being ignited during shotfiring propagated by coal dust. Thirty-five miners were killed.

With the election of a Labour Government in 1945, Clement Attlee succeeded Churchill as Prime Minister and a long sought after programme, from working people and others, for nationalisation, health, welfare and economic reform, including a commitment to full employment, was to radically change the face of Britain in a way which would reflect itself in all aspects of society for decades to come.

# FIFE COUNTY COUNCIL.

EDUCATION COMMITTEE — DUNFERMLINE AREA.

## LAUDER TECHNICAL SCHOOL,
### DUNFERMLINE.

# EVENING CLASSES

SESSION   -   -   1935-36.

Headmaster   -   -   Mr ANDREW R. GEARY, A.T.I.

INTENDING STUDENTS ARE EXPECTED TO ENROL AT THE SCHOOL ON THE EVENINGS OF MONDAY AND TUESDAY, 9TH AND 10TH SEPTEMBER, BETWEEN THE HOURS OF 7 AND 8.

Students enrolling for the first time must bring School Certificates, or other evidence of Attainment, with them when they enrol.

SESSION COMMENCES ON

## MONDAY, 16th September 1935.

### FEES.

| | |
|---|---|
| Article 2 (i.) CLASSES   -   -   -   -   - | No Fee. |
| Article 2 (ii.) SINGLE CLASSES   -   -   -   - | 3/- (Non-Returnable). |
| Article 2 (ii.) COURSES | 5/- (Non-Returnable). |
| Article 2 (iii.) CLASSES | |
| Article 2 (iv.) CLASSES   -   -   -   - | 3/- (Non-Returnable). |

NOTES.—1. Students enrolling in an organised Course at the earliest opportunity after leaving the Day School will be admitted free.

2. Unemployed will be admitted free.

N.B.—Prizes and Certificates will be distributed on Tuesday, 17th September, at 8 p.m. Parents, friends, and all others interested cordially invited.

---

# LAUDER TECHNICAL SCHOOL.

MR JOHN ROBERTSON, HEADMASTER.

*SESSION   -   1915-1916.*

COMMENCING MONDAY, 27TH SEPTEMBER 1915.

## FIFE COUNTY COUNCIL
### EDUCATION COMMITTEE — DUNFERMLINE AREA

# PROSPECTUS OF
## LAUDER TECHNICAL COLLEGE
### DUNFERMLINE
# CONTINUATION CLASSES

### SESSION 1952-53

## CONTENTS

## LAUDER TECHNICAL COLLEGE

| | |
|---|---|
| *Address* | New Row, Dunfermline. |
| *Telephone Number* | Dunfermline 1349. |
| *Principal* | W. STEWART LIDDLE, B.Sc., F.R.I.C. |
| *Deputy Principal* | DAVID D. DEWAR, M.A. |

The College was established in 1899 by Mr Andrew Carnegie in honour of his uncle, Mr George Lauder, a Dunfermline business man. It now comes under the administration of the Education Committee of Fife County Council.

Both Day and Evening Classes are conducted. This Prospectus deals only with Evening Classes. (For information concerning Day Classes, the Principal should be consulted.)

Evening Continuation Classes are organised into Courses and Single Classes. The former cater in the main for apprentices in the Textile, Building, Engineering, and Bakery Trades. The latter are designed to meet the cultural, æsthetic, and miscellaneous needs, or the special requirements, of the general public.

## COLLEGE CALENDAR

| | |
|---|---|
| September 1 (Monday) | Enrolment 7 to 8 p.m. |
| „ 2 (Tuesday) | Enrolment 7 to 8 p.m. |
| „ 8 (Monday) | Classes begin 7 p.m. |
| October 6 (Monday) | Autumn Holiday. |
| December 19 (Friday) | Classes close for Christmas Vacation. |
| January 5 (Monday) | Classes resume. |
| March 30 to April 3 | National Certificate Examinations. |
| April 3 | Session ends. |
| April 24 to May 22 | City and Guilds Examinations. |

Three quite early Lauder Prospectuses dating from session 1915 when the Headmaster was Mr John Robertson through to 1935 with Mr Andrew Geary as Headmaster and on to 1952 by which time the Technical School had become a Technical College and the Headmaster's role became one of a Principal.

# Lauder's Principals

*"No one who fails in teaching the members of his own family is capable of teaching others"*
(Confucius c. 500 B.C.)

## George Lauder

In many ways the most notable of all of Lauder College's Headmasters and Principals throughout its ONE HUNDRED YEARS of proud tradition and history has been the grand old pioneer himself, George Lauder, who all those years ago foresaw the need to introduce free technical education. This as a way of giving the student the practical skills required, and industry the kind of employee so desperately needed to match the ever changing environment.

Putting his skills, and his natural bent for leadership, into practice in the upbringing of his own son and nephew, he demonstrated the wisdom of that great Chinese philosopher, Confucius. In so doing, he set in motion the first examples of two Lauder students as pioneers in a developing world and as living proof that Lauder's education was a fruitful investment, specifically for those two, but in more general terms, for the whole world.

## Dr John MacDonald  MA  BSc PhD

The first baton of Lauder's Legacy was handed to Dr John MacDonald who, at the time of his appointment to the New Lauder Technical School in 1899, was also Rector of its near neighbour, Dunfermline High School. Dr MacDonald became Rector of Dunfermline High School after the resignation of Mr George Dunn B.A., in December, 1898. In those early years the High School operated during the day and Lauder Technical School in the evening.

It was only through the 'fortune of misfortune' that the new Lauder Technical School was to gain such a reputable and capable figure as Dr MacDonald for its first senior appointment. An appointment of one Dr Andrew Thomson in January 1899 never materialised when he declined the post, for personal reasons. MacDonald was proud to accept it.

Dr MacDonald had been Mathematics and Science Master at George Watson's College in Edinburgh, when he was asked if he would be willing to take up the post of Rector of the Dunfermline High School in early 1899 at a salary of £400 per year. It soon became a joint appointment when in October 1899 Lauder Technical School was opened a few feet away from the Dunfermline High School. It was thanks to the personal efforts of Dr MacDonald that the preparations for the opening of the new Lauder School were in place on that grand ceremonial day in October 1899. He worked round the clock the night before, after the classes had all gone home, to ensure that everything was in place for the big day. In 1906 he wrote an article on Dunfermline High School, for the EIS Congress Handbook, in which he was able to trace the origins of the High School back to the foundations of Dunfermline Abbey in 1573. MacDonald later became Director of Studies for Lauder Technical School, and was a most important figure in those early months and years. Imprinting his authority and warm personal character on the classes while the School was in its early stages, he laid a good solid foundation for the next ONE HUNDRED YEARS.

## Mr John Robertson

While Dr MacDonald had been the first senior appointment made at the new Lauder Technical School, it was not long after that a Headmaster was required to cope with the ever increasing workload. Mr John Robertson, a personal friend of Mr George Lauder, was appointed Headmaster of Lauder Technical School, on top of his other duties as Head of the Art Department and Mathematics Instructor, circa 1902.

Mr Robertson began teaching Science and Art classes in an old church hall in Dunfermline in 1881, and became Drawing Master at St Margaret's School prior to joining Lauder Technical School. His Art Classes were designed to carry the student on to a more advanced degree from the Elementary School; also, to serve for the further instruction of Teachers in the Elementary Schools.

Lauder submitted the following motion on 3 July 1882 to the School Board: *"That Mr Robertson, the present Art Master in Dunfermline, should be furnished with the West Room in the old Commercial School that he should be appointed Drawing Master to the Board that his duties shall be to attend to all the pupil teachers in the Board Schools once or twice a week at a salary to be afterwards fixed."*
It was unanimously agreed to allow Mr Robertson the use of the West Room in the old Commercial School for drawing classes on the same terms upon which he was allowed the use of the High School. This was at a time when the School Board had given permission to use Lauder Technical School for 'Teachers' Saturday classes.

By 1909-1910 Mr Robertson, with his assistant Peter S Black, seems to have been quite instrumental in developing and expanding day and evening classes as well as the staff during his term of leadership, bringing in new and varied courses to match the requirements of industry:

| SUBJECT ENROLLED | TEACHER | PUPILS |
| --- | --- | --- |
| Science and Art | John Robertson | 83 |
| Weaving | Thomas Milne | 51 |
| Mathematics | P.S.Black | 144 |
| Chemistry | R.Somerville | 10 |
| Electricity & Magnetism | T. Watters | 23 |
| Electrical Engineering | R. Barr | 36 |
| Mining | J. Parker | 427* |
| Plumbing | R. Robertson | 30 |
| Building Construction | Nichol Selkirk | 63 |
| Engineering | G. M. Hamilton | 84 |

| | | |
|---|---|---|
| English Course | John Morris | 13 |
| Commercial Course | Peter Stormonth | 12 |
| Shorthand | Peter Stormonth | 10 |
| Book-keeping | Peter Stormonth | 12 |
| Sick Nursing & Laws of Health | Rachel S. Ogilvie | 28 |
| Needlework | Helen Morton | 22 |
| Millinery | Jessie Brough | 32 |
| Dressmaking | Jessie Cuthbert | 43 |
| Laundry | Edith Hagen | 37 |

* Joseph Parker also worked at the Mining School at Cowdenbeath.

Mr Nichol Selkirk, who was a teacher in the Building Construction and Carpentry and Joinery Classes at the Lauder Technical School, from 1905 to 1915 wrote of his experiences under the Headmaster, Mr John Robertson:

*"At this time the Building Classes met on the Ground Floor of the School, two rooms, separated by a "Blackboard" partition. The Headmaster was Mr John Robertson. I cannot speak too highly of Mr Robertson during my time at the "Lauder": I had only to ask for supplies for the classes and got them straight away. He also got my Examination papers printed for me on hand when I reached Dunfermline from my home in Edinburgh."*

## Mr William S Byres  BSc

Mr William Byres began his twenty two-year career at Lauder Technical School as Teacher of Mathematics and Science in 1921. Mr Byres was appointed by the 'Area Committee' composed of the local members of the Education Authority. Writing of his memories of Lauder in 1961, Byres recalled:

*"Well do I remember one question they asked me at the interview;*
*"Can you work a donkey engine?"*

Mr Byres continued as Teacher of Maths & Science until 1929 when he was appointed Headmaster of Lauder Technical School that same year. His monthly salary was £110 and two deputies were appointed to take duty on one evening each at a salary of £25. At this time the monthly salary for the staff was approximately £500 paid out in loose cash over a weekly period. When Byres applied to the Education Authority for salary envelopes an official turned the request down. However, the Director and Treasurer overturned the decision and within a short time the staff were paid by cheque. Lauder Technical School was the first School to be paid in this way.

Byres remembered the lack of proper facilities for practical work:

*"At the final City and Guilds Examination in Plumbing the students were required to bend iron pipes round a telegraph pole in the school playground."*

Although Byres was not Headmaster for a great many years, he did a tremendous amount of work. He wrote:

*"My three years as Headmaster of the School can only be described as hectic. I had a very full programme at the School, a considerable amount of extra-curricular work, mostly during the summer term, and the expanding evening school required my attendance on most evenings of the week."*

Details of the Lauder School Departments with their principal teachers while Mr Byres was Headmaster:

| SUBJECT | TEACHER |
|---|---|
| Building and Construction | William Millar & John Burt |
| Engineering | James Black |
| Textiles | A. R. Geary & Henry Cook |

This was the only department with day-release students

| | |
|---|---|
| Breadmaking and Confectionery | Thomas Ness; Robert Beveridge & Alex Rhynd |

 A feature of this course was the annual exhibition of work judged for many years by Messrs, Lighbody & Stuart of Buckhaven

| Art | A. McMorland | General Art |
|---|---|---|
| | Robert Morris | Design |
| | D W Gunn | Life Drawing |

Also:

| | |
|---|---|
| Pharmacy | Classes in Chemistry & Physics preparing for part 1 of the professional examination. |
| Hairdressing | Well attended classes for members of the trade, with the same two teachers coming from Edinburgh for a number of years. |
| Adult Education | In 1930, Professors & Lecturers from St Andrews gave a series of lectures under the heading "Man and His World". The enrolment was well over 200 and attendances were well maintained. |
| Plumbing | Mr Thomas Pye<br>Alex Duncan |
| Painting and Decorating | D Marshall<br>Daniel Syme |

Mr Byres enjoyed his three-year term as Headmaster and gained much valuable experience through it.

*"I resigned from the Headmastership on being appointed Principal Teacher of Mathematics in Dunfermline High School but agreed to act as deputy to Mr Geary at the request of the Director of Education",* said Mr Byres.

## Mr Andrew R Geary ATI

Dunfermline was still world famous for its textile industry by the time Andrew R Geary took up the position of Textile Teacher, on a part-time evening work basis, at the Textile School (the same campus as Lauder Technical School) following the opening of the new School Extension in 1910. At a meeting of the Fife Education Authority in April 1923, in connection with Day Classes at Dunfermline Textile School, it was recommended that a 'full-time' teacher be appointed, *"preferably with Belfast experience."*

The post of 'Teacher of Weaving' at Dunfermline Textile School was advertised following the death of the Weaving Teacher Thomas Milne, at a salary of £350 per year; Andrew Geary was appointed to his own post on a full-time basis; possibly with the approval of Mr Anderson, then Headmaster of the Continuation Classes at the Textile School.

The quality of the education at the Textile School, which was of the finest and of the highest quality in the country, was largely due to the expertise and contribution of Andrew Geary a native from Belfast, Northern Ireland.

In a report to the Fife Education Committee on October 16th, 1923 Mr A. R. Geary, Teacher of Weaving classes at Dunfermline Textile School stated his concerns:

*"(a) That in the afternoon classes there was a minimum attendance of 18 pupils.*
*(b) That in the evening classes the enrolment was 38 in the first year; 8 in the third and 3 in the fourth year."*

With such numbers Mr Geary did not think it possible to impart adequate "practical" instruction and he therefore suggested the appointment of an assistant teacher or tenter. He also maintained that the machinery required much attention in order that it might be maintained in satisfactory working order. Mr Geary's report was approved generally, and it was agreed that the Convenor and Mr Somerville investigate and report with regard to the application for an assistant teacher or tenter.

A letter from the Administration Clerk dated 28th November 1923 gave the go-ahead for the temporary appointment of Mr Robert Thomson, janitor of the Textile School, as mechanical assistant to Mr Geary, Weaving Teacher, for an extra payment of ten shillings (50p) per week.

Alexander Geary served as Textile Teacher, in the Textile School, for many years before being appointed Headmaster of the Textile School in 1923, taking over from a Mr Anderson. In 1927, the Textile School was merged with the Lauder Technical School. Mr Geary eventually became Headmaster of the merged establishment in 1932, and this position he held for the long period of time until 1951. He operated from a room in the Textile Building which he used as his office and, as the bulk of the classes operated in the evenings, the Headmaster would often have to move out of his "office" so that a class could be held there.

Throughout his career, Mr Geary had been in charge of Lauder Technical School during some of the most difficult years in history. Even throughout these difficulties many Lauder students who entered for examinations of the City and Guilds of London Institute gained no fewer than 1,568 certificates and, for especially good examination results, one gold medal, 21 silver medals and 13 bronze medals.

Mr Geary eventually retired in 1951 and pursued his passion for the game of golf which he was known to enjoy immensely.

## William Stewart Liddle  BSc FRIC

Stewart Liddle, a native of Dundee, was appointed first 'Principal' (as it became) of Lauder Technical School in 1951 and presided over some of the greatest changes in the College's proud ONE HUNDRED year history. Liddle took over at a time of countrywide expansion of Further Education following the Second World War. The 'College' as Mr Liddle (and Mr Lauder) preferred to call it, greatly diversified the range of courses available notably into Catering and Commercial or Secretarial Studies, which increased the intake of female students. Accommodation for these classes, like many classes that were to spring up under Liddle, became a problem and operated out of former school premises in the Wilson Institute on New Row, which date back to 1859.

The former Canmore Primary School was also used by converting the premises into a motor vehicle workshop and a Bakery. The former High School building was ultimately used to house the College administration and Commercial Department together with two large rooms devoted to the intensive training of sewing machinists on industrial sewing machines.

When Liddle was appointed Principal in 1951 there were three full-time members on the staff, including himself. By 1960 there were 13, and in 1968 members had risen to 50. The extension of day-release and the introduction and development of full-time courses were two major developments during his seventeen years in office. He saw the increase in the number of non-vocational classes, which came under the College jurisdiction, grow at a rate which far outpaced that of non-vocational education in Scotland. His flair for innovation also brought the College to a far wider public attention than had ever been done previously.

When Liddle began in 1951 there were no full-time students and approximately 100 part-time students. The emphasis was almost completely on evening classes with day classes being confined to day release in building and textiles. With Queen Anne School then in occupation, the available accommodation during the day was limited to an annex in Bothwell Street for building, and to one room, one laboratory and the weaving shed in the Textile building. When Woodmill Junior High School, then in its formative stages, succeeded Queen Anne as the day-time tenants of the building half of the accommodation was freed for further education purposes. The transfer of Woodmill to its new premises in 1960 gave the College virtually exclusive use of the buildings both for day and evening classes. This development had been preceded by the equipping of the Wilson Institute as a bakery; the building of a new engineering block adjacent to the Old High building, and by the extensive renovation of the Building Department annex at Bothwell Street.

Further developments under Liddle's leadership included the take over in 1961 of the evening continuation classes at Dunfermline High School.

Mr Liddle collaborated enthusiastically with the Carnegie Dunfermline Trust when the Craft School in Viewfield Terrace, a Carnegie benefaction of long standing administered by the Trust, came under joint Authority/Trust control. Mr Liddle also encouraged courses in 'Preparation for Retirement' covering the topics likely to be encountered on retirement which brings with it problems associated with excess of leisure and a reduction of income. It was the first College outside Glasgow to make this provision and was probably the only course in the country in which the Principal was an enrolled student!

The amount of effort and sheer hard work Mr Liddle put into the consolidation, extension and development of Lauder College can be glimpsed, in a letter he sent to Mr Alex Ritchie in June 1961:

*" I must apologise for not replying sooner to your last letter, and plead in extenuation that the advent of Commonwealth Technical Training Week with its attendant functions, College Exhibition and weeks of preparation and administration, the new courses for Session 1961 - 62, and the detailed preliminary estimates of accommodation required for the new College to be built, together with the normal routine work and the inevitable crop of emergencies have constituted an avalanche which has all but submerged me.*

*In consequence of all this my clerkesses are loaded with work, my office a shambles, my wife a widow, my children orphans, my garden a wilderness, and if I don't get a holiday soon, I shall out-rival the Hesperus."*

Stewart Liddle assumed the Principalship of Cowdenbeath Technical College in 1967, when the two Colleges amalgamated but retained the Lauder name.

The Principal of Cowdenbeath Technical College, William John Morris, transferred in a similar capacity to Kirkcaldy Technical College and became responsible for the formation of the Scottish Association of Principals, of which he became its first convenor. Liddle also played a major part in establishing regular meetings of the Principals of the Fife Technical Colleges, which played its part in encouraging the formation of the larger body.

Outwith academic matters there were two projects which greatly occupied Mr Liddle and to which he paid meticulous attention, each of which helped to enhance the standing of the College and bring it to a wider public notice. The first was the design and production of the College crest and the second was the motto which symbolised Lauder for many years, and to which he devoted considerable thought. He determined that each feature would have relevance to the College.

There is an amusing postscript to this story. The use of a crest by any institution is governed by the constraints of heraldry and the authority for design and display lies in the power of the Lord Lyon King of Arms. However, having designed the crest to his own satisfaction, Mr Liddle proceeded to have it displayed on the College stationery. On reflection, however, he considered it would be prudent to obtain official approval. He composed a letter on the subject but unfortunately his secretary prepared it on the headed notepaper with the crest instead of on plain paper as instructed. In a rare lapse of concentration Mr Liddle signed the missive and off it went to the Lord Lyon. The reply was immediate and most intimidating. Sir Thomas Innes of Learney, perhaps mistaking an oversight for impertinence issued a statement of the dire penalties incurred by the display and use of an unauthorised crest or coat of arms. Further, it was for the Lord Lyon to design the crest, the applicant being supposed to indicate only the desired features. This was a bad start to the new crest and probably delayed the final authorisation. The fee for the crest was suspected to have been paid by Liddle himself.

Stewart Liddle took up his post two years after the College Jubilee in 1949, an event which passed without celebration or without record of an event. Had Liddle been in post this would not have happened for he believed in the value of such occasions to bring the College to wider public notice, which he did on the 150th anniversary of the birth of George Lauder (1815) on 31st May, 1965 planning long, hard and in some style, for the celebration of the sesquincentenary. Andrew Carnegie's daughter, Mrs Margaret Carnegie Miller was enthusiastic about the project and for the occasion donated the portrait of George Lauder by the artist Charles Mackie which hung in the Carnegie Scottish holiday home at Skibo Castle for 60 years.

Latterly, Stewart Liddle represented the Dunfermline and West Fife Chamber of Commerce at meetings of the Education and Training Committee of the Edinburgh Chamber and on the Education Committee of the Council of Scottish Chambers of Commerce.

Mr Liddle resolved to write a comprehensive history of the College in his retirement and to this end amassed a considerable amount of material. Sadly, however, he was not granted a long retirement and his untimely death and the loss of most of his material meant that the College history is not as full as it might have been - or as he would have wished.

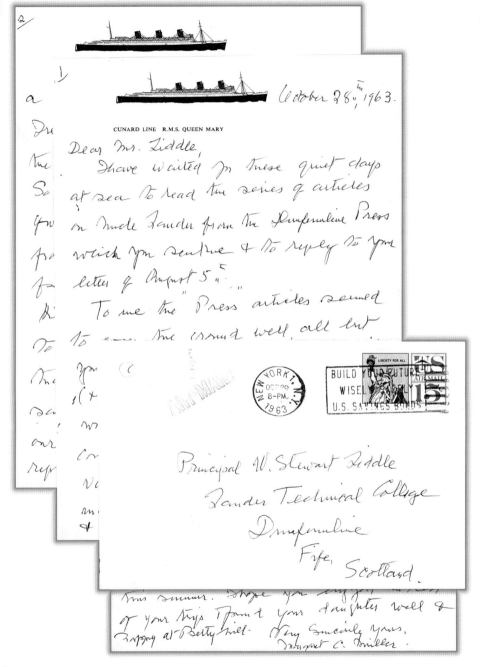

**CUNARD LINE R.M.S. QUEEN MARY**

October 28th, 1963.

Dear Mr. Liddle,

I have waited for these quiet days at sea to read the series of articles on Uncle Lauder from the Dunfermline Press which you sent me & to reply to your letter of August 5th.

To me the "Press" articles seemed to ... the crowd well, all but

Principal W. Stewart Liddle
Lauder Technical College
Dunfermline
Fife, Scotland

this summer. Hope you enjoyed all of your trip. I found your daughter well & happy at Betty Hill. Very sincerely yours,
Margaret C. Miller.

Another of the many letters sent to Principal Liddle from Margaret Carnegie Miller. On this occasion, writing from the Cunard Line, the Queen Mary, she recalls her experiences of old George Lauder and how so very special he was to her father Andrew Carnegie.

## Matthew Ian Andrews BSc MInstP

Stewart Liddle retired in 1968 and was succeeded by Mr Ian Andrews who became Principal of the existing Lauder and Cowdenbeath Technical Colleges. Mr Andrews had been Depute Principal from 1964-1968 and took over at a time when construction of the new Lauder College at Halbeath had begun. He therefore had the privilege of overseeing the transfer of Lauder College to its new site which opened in 1970. His first task was two-fold – to promote a feeling of unity among staff located in two main centres some miles apart and to prepare for the move to the first phase of the new construction at Halbeath.

There was also the question of the day-to-day operation of the complex and for this he was fortunate to have the services of two very able Depute Principals, Mr John Barclay and Mr Peter Richardson of Cowdenbeath and Dunfermline respectively. These gentlemen operated this for the eight year period between 1968 until the construction at Halbeath was completed. The physical integration commenced in 1970 when the first phase of the new construction brought together the Engineering Departments, together with the Mining Department from Cowdenbeath. The process was completed in 1975 when the remaining College Departments came together at Halbeath.

A native of Glasgow, Mr Andrews was educated at the local school, Shawlands Academy (1929-41), proceeding to Glasgow University to study for an Honours Degree in Physics. There he enrolled in an Admiralty scheme to recruit Radar Officers for the Royal Navy in which he served 1943-47 in a variety of appointments ashore and afloat. Returning to University, he graduated in 1949 and then took teacher training at Jordanhill College in Glasgow; after teaching physics in secondary schools Mr Andrews commenced his career in Further Education in 1953 when he took up a post of Lecturer in

Physics at Paisley Technical College (now Paisley University). His next post was Head of Department of Mathematics and Physics at Kilmarnock Technical College in 1958 from where he came with his wife and young family to Dunfermline on his appointment as Depute to Principal Stewart Liddle at Lauder in 1964.

The sixties and seventies, with Andrews as Depute and later as Principal, were a period of great activity and general expansion, with the exception sadly of Lauder Textile Department which suffered inevitably with the decline in that period of the long established Dunfermline linen and latterly silk factories. The number of students fell very seriously during this period and the Scottish Education Department closed the Department in 1968. The staff involved were re-deployed, the senior lecturer and one other to the Scottish College of Textiles at Galashiels, a Central Institution under Department control. Two others were given retraining in other disciplines.

In 1970, as news came through of a hold-up in the building of the new College at the Halbeath site, designed to consolidate College operations, Mr Andrews drew attention to the conditions, national and local, in which the College was continuing to operate:

*"Nationally"*, said Mr Andrews, *"further education is in a state of uncertainty as circumstances alter, not always reflecting the forecasts of a few years ago. Future developments, short and long-term, cast their shadow before them. Locally, activities were conducted in six main centres, two in Dunfermline, one in Cowdenbeath, two in Lochgelly and one in Kelty"*. Some of the courses were operating in buildings which Mr Andrews described as, *"virtually slums, condemned schools"*. He regretted that the programme was caught in the, then, present financial climate. *"Apart from the obvious disadvantages which such geographical scatter entails, mitigating against a feeling of corporate student life, conditions in some, or all, of these centres were scarcely conducive to the high standards of attainment which were achieved. The unusual features of continuing amalgamation of two previously separate Colleges and the transfer of certain courses and associated staff, combined with normal transfers and promotions, saw an unusually high reduction in total teaching staff of the order of 20% to 78 full-time members."*

Mr Andrews pointed to the progress which had been made in the field of adult and non-vocational education with the appointment of Mr George Metcalfe,

Tutor-Organiser, whose enthusiasm laid firm foundations for closer links with the community. *"It is this closer liaison between the towns and the College, in its widest sense, that I welcome very much indeed,"* he said.

Mr Andrews succeeded in steering the College through one of the most difficult periods in its ONE HUNDRED year history and put it on a sure footing, with more community outreach involvement, for the remainder of the century.

### Mr John Lisgo BSc Econ

Principal Andrews retired in 1983 and was succeeded by Mr John Lisgo, a native of Durham, who took up his post as Principal of Lauder Technical College on August 22nd, 1983. Mr Lisgo attended Robert Richardson's Grammar school in Ryhope, near Sunderland. His further education was completed at the London School of Economics. Following his three years there, he completed a Diploma in Education at Durham University.

Mr Lisgo began his career in education as a teacher of mathematics and history at Durham's Boldon Secondary School. His next post, in 1963, was at the Monkwearmouth College of Further Education, Sunderland, as a lecturer in economics. He later became the Liaison Officer for Adult Education at the College. In 1972, Mr Lisgo moved north of the Border to take up a post as a Senior Lecturer in Social Studies at Edinburgh's Stevenson College. Three years later, he became head of the Language and Social Studies Department and, in 1980, he became Assistant Principal.

At Stevenson College, John Lisgo had been involved in the growth of trade union studies. He also helped to develop these studies when he came to Lauder which already had a well-established Trade Union Studies Department with a national reputation under the leadership of Mike Morris.

Under Ian Andrews stewardship the College had secured its place in the community. John Lisgo determined to see it evolve further as a resource for the people and public of Dunfermline. One feature of this work was the introduction of government funded programmes for the long term unemployed, an area of work which was to develop the College's skills and strengths throughout the eighties and nineties.

Mr Lisgo was keen to develop outreach activity, which became a feature under previous principal Mr Andrews. Littlewoods store in Dunfermline was the scene of one of the new ideas presided over by Mr Lisgo in May 1984 when the then Grand Slam rugby hero Jim Aitken added his support to a Lauder Technical College scheme designed to encourage the public to consider further education courses.

Jim who led the Scottish team to their Triple Crown and Grand Slam victories in the Five Nations Championship, opened the Lauder exhibition at the Littlewoods store and was made an honorary member of the College for his efforts as well as receiving a clock from Principal Lisgo. In return he presented the College with a signed rugby ball. Visitors to the exhibition, situated at the entrance doors to the shop, were able to use the video and computer equipment on show to plan their College course from "modules." Mr Lisgo said:

*"The College is part of the community and it is a resource to which we want to alert people. We are hoping the exhibition will attract more people to come into the College."*

Mr Lisgo's term of office at Lauder was very short and he left in 1986 to take up an appointment at an Edinburgh College.

### Dr Alan Brown  BSc PhD

The next Principal of Lauder Technical College, Dr Alan Brown was at his desk and ready to go in mid May, weeks before he was officially due to start his new post as Principal. Dr Brown officially began as Principal of Lauder College on June 22nd 1987. He said:

*" I saw Lauder College at the time of applying for the job. I liked the area and thought it was a good development to my career. There are numerous challenges facing further education, the greatest of which is to be responsive and offer a greater range of opportunities to people. In connection with that, we have got to become client centred by discussing with a variety of people, employers, trade unions, schools and the general public, what their needs are and how we can best meet them. A dialogue has to be developed."*

Dr Brown capped seven years of study at Glasgow University with BSc honours degree and a PhD. After holding various teaching posts in Ayrshire, he became Depute Director of Education with Berwick County Council in 1972 remaining as Assistant Director of Education with Borders Regional Council after regionalisation.

The leadership which Dr Brown provided became a valuable asset during the changing climate where students became customers and an emphasis was given to income generating courses. This culminated in the award to the College in 1993 of BS 5750 for quality systems, the first College in Scotland to earn this prestigious award. Dr Brown began the extension of the work done at the College to design on-site training for individual companies. One example of this approach allowed a Fife building company to save time and money by arranging for College lecturers to train their workforce at building sites. By seconding a number of his 142 lecturers to industry and commerce periodically, Dr Brown enabled them to keep up to date in practice as well as in theory.

In the end every student is an individual and individual human stories have always been a part of life at Lauder College. Dr Brown recalled how one blind student enrolled at the College, studied for O' grades and then went on to take Highers. After a further course at Lauder College, the student ended up with a well-paid job in local government.

Dr Brown was involved nationally in the move of Further Education Colleges from Regional Council control to direct control at incorporation which took place in 1993. In that same year a report by HM Inspectors of Schools said that *"the quality of teaching and learning at Lauder College was of an exceptionally high standard."*

A special tribute was paid to Dr Brown's leadership which had led to "effective, confident and open" management. At the time of inspection there were 5,000 individual students, of whom 739 were full-time, and they were achieving very satisfactory success rates.

During the period immediately preceding the incorporation in 1993, Mr Peter Richardson was appointed Acting Principal, to enable Dr Brown to prepare the College for incorporation. Peter Richardson retired in 1993, after a long and distinguished career at Lauder College and in the further education service.

Unfortunately Dr Brown had to retire at the end of 1995 on health grounds and was succeeded by Ms Janet Lowe who had been Depute Principal of Lauder since 1993.

The College motto of "Tak Tent Briz Yont" old Scots for "Take Stock To Move Forward" was never more in evidence than under the guidance and leadership of Dr Alan Brown.

## Ms Janet Lowe  BA (Hons) MBA MIPD

When Janet Lowe took up post in January 1996 she was one of only two women Principals, and the first woman to lead the College founded in honour of George Lauder. An experienced manager with a background in higher education, she brought a new perspective to further education, and a new outlook for Lauder College.

The first three years of her principalship have been bold and imaginative, characterised by her commitment and professionalism. A firm believer in the principles of public service and stewardship, Ms Lowe has strengthened Carnegie's legacy and put Lauder College at the forefront of further education in Scotland.

Because of her vision the College has broken the bounds of local geography whilst still holding true to its values of quality, service and community development. The College has opened premises across central Scotland, with a presence in Edinburgh, Stirling, Falkirk, Galashiels and the town centre of Dunfermline. A welcome return was also made to Cowdenbeath in 1996 when the College opened its construction training facility – the Woodend Campus.

As a result of Ms Lowe's drive and initiative the College has emerged as a model of enterprise and innovation as well as a centre of excellence. This entrepreneurial approach is something of which Andrew Carnegie would have approved, and has recently resulted in Ms Lowe overseeing the building of a brand new Business Learning Centre on the College campus at Halbeath.

A dedicated ambassador for the College, Ms Lowe has nurtured the College's links with business and industry, and serves on several external bodies, most notably Scottish Enterprise. Her stature and influence in Scotland were recently recognised by her inclusion by Scotland on Sunday newspaper as one of Scotland's fifty most influential women. The College's ability to respond to the needs of business and industry has flourished under Janet Lowe's vision and guidance.

As an Investor in People with a recognised customer focus and a business like approach to the delivery of education and training, Lauder College is now well placed to continue its proud tradition into the next millennium under the leadership of its present Principal.

Janet Lowe                    Gordon Brown M.P

Gordon Brown M.P formally opens the Cowdenbeath Campus - 14th February 1997.

Mr Stewart Liddle (far left) played a large part in establishing regular meetings of the Principals of the Fife Technical Colleges; a development which played its part in encouraging the formation of a larger body which became the Scottish branch of the Assocation of Principals of Technical Institutions of which Liddle was a founder member.
From left to right: W S Liddle, Bett, Newlands, Hogan, Campbell, Martin, Cunningham, Henry, Garner, Hepburn, Ryder, Morris, Hughes, McLeod, Pearce.

# Through the Post-War Years

Winston Churchill was heading his first peacetime Government at the age of seventy-six. War-time rationing was still in operation, though it would be phased out by 1954 and, although signs of austerity looked to be at an end, a report from Europe suggested that Britain's economy was in crisis. Scotland's Stone of Destiny was eventually found in Arbroath after it was stolen from Westminster Abbey. Meanwhile, George Lauder's fifty year old College continued to expand to cope with greater demand.

As the days of Alexander Geary as Headmaster drew to a close at Lauder Technical School, a new chapter was about to begin with the introduction of a new Principal, a Principal who would have a profound effect on the future of Lauder College throughout the fifties and beyond.

A warning that technical education could be overdone and that students also needed to learn to become efficient citizens was given to Lauder students by Mr James Wilkie, Secretary of the Carnegie United Kingdom Trust in January 1950, at a prize-giving ceremony which followed on the heels of the fiftieth anniversary of Lauder Technical School. He paid high tribute to the work done in the Lauder Technical School and especially the outstanding achievements of Malcolm T McAuley, who gained first place in Britain at the intermediate examination for silk and rayon weaving.

Mr Wilkie concluded by saying to those who had been successful and unsuccessful alike *"It was a reflection on the conditions under which the examination was taken that separated those who gained the certificate and those who didn't manage it. To face the burden of two or three hours study after a days work in the workshop or factory demanded some real positive virtue - a toughness of fibre - and to find the going a bit hard was not to be taken as discouragement. To have made an attempt under those conditions was praise enough."*

Accompanying the reorganisation of the Scottish Gas Board in the late 1950s Dunfermline was chosen as a principal centre in the Central Division of Scotland for gas manufacture and distribution. Lauder Technical College was selected as the educational centre for Fife, Stirling and Clackmannan and although the textile industry had received a number of sharp set-backs, it was still fighting to secure new markets. A further development was the introduction of a course in radio service work, leading to a City and Guilds Certificate in radio, for those who were employed in this "young and growing" industry.

The possibility of the name of Lauder Technical School being changed to that of College was first suggested by Councillor John Allan, Dunfermline Convenor of the County Further Education Sub-Committee, as he introduced Mr Stewart Liddle, the new Headmaster, to the staff and students of the school in October 1951. Mr Allan spoke of the regulations dealing with the subject of technical education and said that the Further Education Sub-Committee were suggesting to the parent body that the names of the four technical schools in Fife should be changed to Colleges, and that headmasters should be known as Principals. Mr Allan went on to speak of the high standards set by the Lauder Technical School in the sphere of technical education, and paid tribute to the work of the former headmaster, Mr Alexander Geary. Mr Liddle was pleased to know that the name of the Lauder Technical School would be changed to that of Lauder Technical College. He praised his predecessor for keeping the Lauder flag flying high and pointed out that the pupils were no longer to be referred to as pupils but students.

For over thirty years the Education Committee had been dependent on the kindness of local bakers for the use of their premises for the teaching and training of young apprentices. In September 1953, Mr Philip Douglas, Managing Secretary of Dunfermline Co-operative Society Ltd, was proud to officially open the College bakery in the Wilson Institute in New Row. *"It was a particularly progressive step in the education of bakery students in Fife,"* said Mr Urquhart, Chairman of the Dunfermline District Education Committee of Fife County Council.

Now they had a bakery under the direct control of the Principal which would make the College entirely independent of any bakery, allowing the students to do much more practical work. The bakery opened four nights weekly and, in addition, there was a special class for cake design and decorating.

The "machine age" had arrived and developments were described as "almost staggering" at the annual prize giving of students in February 1955. The comments came from Mr T H Davidson, Principal of a Dundee firm of brass founders and textile consultants. Referring to the tremendous developments which had taken place since the war, he highlighted developments in textile machinery as an example of this. Of the opportunities in technical education Mr Davidson said: *"The facilities which had existed in my young day were but a 'fleabite' compared with those available to-day."* The equipment he had seen at Lauder Technical College led him to urge the students to make full use of the opportunity provided by these installations. *"Because of the developments of "the machine," young men now required a higher standard of skill and knowledge to meet the demands of industry. The faster the machine went the more maintenance it required and thus the more mechanical knowledge was demanded. This was now possible in the technical College of today"* said Mr Davidson, congratulating the Principal, Mr Liddle, and the staff on their results achieved in the College. To those who had not been successful, Mr Davidson said that the only thing a man could reprimand himself for was failing to do his best. *"The teacher cannot ask for more than that"* he said.

Mr Urquhart, Chairman of Dunfermline District Education Sub-Committee, said *"the results of last year showed that the College had won a silver medal and two bronze medals in external examinations. Seven preliminary certificates, 21 intermediate, and 27 final certificates had been gained, and other successes brought the total certificates won to 63. A most credible performance on the part of the students. The Education Committee liked to think that Fife was now the most progressive county in Scotland so far as technical education was concerned."*

A new engineering block containing electrical and heat engine laboratories and engineering workshop, along with staff rooms and offices was yet another extension of Lauder Technical College, the building of which began in November 1953. It was opened in October 1955 and housed the very latest types of equipment including individual desks and strip roof lighting, a new concept for the fifties. Most of the flooring in the block was supplied by the Edinburgh firm Semtex Ltd.

The variety of courses available to students at the Lauder Technical College was illustrated in an attractive prospectus prepared for the 1955-56 session in which Principal Liddle detailed the facilities, buildings and equipment which he said were continuing to be extended every year.

By then the College was made up of six main buildings. The Lauder Building in Priory Lane contained an assembly hall, lecture and drawing rooms, physics and chemistry laboratories and joiners and painters workshops.

The Textile Building in New Row included a lecture, drawing and sewing room and a plumbing workshop. Its principal feature was provision for the teaching of linen, silk and rayon weaving for which it was equipped with a weaving shed and a textile testing department, furnished with the most up-to-date facilities. The Wilson Building in New Row was equipped for breadmaking, flour, confectionery, cake decoration and cookery classes, while the Gymnasium in Priory Lane was available for classes in physical training and country dancing.

The Engineering extension in Priory Lane, opened in 1955, housed engineering laboratories and workshops as well as the College office. As an adjunct to the College there was the Wightman Building at Bothwell Street which contained lecture rooms and workshops for joiners, bricklayers, slaters, painters and decorators. It was the centre for day-release classes in building.

Lauder Technical College also provided day courses in addition to evening continuation classes. The day-release courses, which Lauder Technical College had pioneered since 1910, were provided free, apprentices being released by their employers, usually for one day a week, with pay. Dinner was provided if required at a cost of one shilling (5p) and travelling expenses were refunded subject to certain conditions.

Day courses were mainly provided for trainees in the textile industry and building trades. The textile courses were designed to meet the needs of the local textile industry, including linen, silk and rayon weaving with specialisation in damasks. Further study was available at evening classes for 3rd, 4th, 5th and in some cases 6th year students. At the evening classes there was an almost unlimited variety of courses and single-subject courses, the latter of which was dependent on the number of enrolments. The courses were normally carried on over 26 weeks. They included courses leading to National Certificates, to City and Guilds, and to other nationally recognised qualifications. Lauder, like other Colleges in Fife and Lothian, was affiliated to one Central Institution – Heriot-Watt College in Edinburgh.

By 1953 there were still no full-time day classes. The various courses that were in operation were planned to prepare students for national certificates and City and Guilds examinations.

The freeing of accommodation at the Lauder Technical College by the transfer of Queen Anne School and later Woodmill School, which had been operating out of the old Dunfermline High, to their own new premises, enabled Lauder to take possession of the whole educational complex. Even then the accommodation was not only outdated, but inadequate to cope with the rapid growth in demand for technical education.

The first stage in Lauder's programme of development was highlighted in 1955 by the opening of the 'John Allan' Building, named after the Convenor of the County Further Education Sub Committee. The second stage was signalled by the completion of reconstruction of the Wightman Building in Bothwell Street in 1957. A third stage saw the freeing from occupation by school pupils of two additional buildings on the New Row and Priory Lane site, namely Canmore Buildings and the Textile Buildings. Tenancy of the former building enabled the College to proceed with long overdue developments in breadmaking and flour confectionery. A fourth stage was initiated by the completion of the new Woodmill School building in 1960 which now ensured the unrestricted entry of the College into the remaining educational buildings on the site, the Lauder Building, the old High School Building and the Wilson Institute. Further stages were to see the integration of existing buildings into a unified Technical College.

A call to employers to release their best workmen for teaching and to allow their apprentices to attend day-release classes was made by the Rev T R Gardener MA, when he presented the prizes at the Ceremony held in October 1956. Mr Gardener, who spoke as a member of the Further Education Sub-Committee of Fife Education Committee, said that the newspapers had been featuring news about the "teddy boys" gangs, but he wished they would tell the public about the "T–Square" boys, for it was these lads who were going to put the country in the forefront. Mr Gardener said that it was a long, long time since it could be said with any confidence *"Britannia rules the waves"*. They had to realise that it was technical Colleges and the resultant workmanship that had created that position and maintained it. He then went on to make a suggestion which would have had Andrew Carnegie and George Lauder turning in their grave, not to mention the disapproval of the Principal, Mr Liddle. Mr Gardener hoped that when all of the College developments were completed that the Lauder College would become known as the *"Royal Technical College of Dunfermline."*

In November 1956, a pre-National Service meeting was held in the Canmore Building of the Lauder Technical College, the first meeting of its kind to be held in Dunfermline for young men who were required to register for National Service. The purpose of the meeting was to give those who were about to begin their two year period of National Service some idea of what branches of the service they could enter.

There was for various reasons during the fifties, including National Service, a general problem of getting the amount of day release students that were eligible to attend Lauder from employers. However Fife County Council, in order to put pressure on employers, had decided on a policy that no employer who refused to allow his apprentices to attend day-release classes would get any contracting work from the Council.

Lauder's new Building Centre at Bothwell Street was completed in March 1957 and, at an estimated cost of £17,000, it was capable of holding some 400 students weekly. The centre provided practical and theoretical training for day-release apprentices who got one day a week off to attend classes. When it opened, the centre had a staff of two full-time instructors who were getting good co-operation from the students' employers. Ten double benches with storage space and provision for left handed workers formed part of the new facilities in the Centre.

In 1955 Lauder provided eleven rooms for day students. By 1958 this had risen to 26 rooms. By 1960 students were operating out of 46 rooms and the staffing reached a high of thirteen full-time teachers as well as one hundred part-time teachers.

From 1945 the tasks facing the country had been enormous and the level of expectations from the Scottish people very high. Since 1946 the British Government had nationalised the Coal Mines and had taken over control of various transport and communications services, as well as the supply of electricity. The Government was about to extend their nationalisation programme. By 1960, short term economic policies gave way to a new interest in long-term Government planning. By the early 1960s the Government had introduced several long-term plans, including a programme for building ninety new hospitals over ten years and a six-year scheme for the development of roads and motorways costing £1,000,000,000.

The Local Employment Act 1960 meant that companies setting up new industries in Fife were eligible for assistance. Any firm building a factory within a designated area received a 25% grant towards the building cost and a 10% grant towards the installation of the plant. Firms coming into Fife were able to obtain Government finance to defray the cost of training local labour. Lauder Technical College, while being well placed to take advantage of new and expanding industries and to train local labour with the new skills necessary for these industries, still operated out of inadequate and geographically scattered premises. It was a problem in which the Education Committee was only too aware. At the annual Lauder prize-giving ceremony in October 1960 Convenor of Fife Education Committee, John Allan, used the occasion to highlight plans to consolidate all of Lauder's teaching operations into completely new premises within Fife. The only problem they faced was where to house a new Lauder Technical College.

In 1965, Principal Liddle, in presenting a summary of the work and achievements of the College during the session 1964-65, explained that there had been some slackening off in the exceptionally high rate of expansion of the College which had been the characteristic of the previous five years. The development of pre-vocational courses had been slower than expected and there had been a further shift of emphasis from evening classes to day release. Experiments on the release of pupils from secondary schools to attend the College for vocational instruction had proved successful. Session 1964-65 had seen the start of further experiments which would ultimately lead to a new system of pre-vocational education in which the pupils of all secondary schools would in their final year at school attend College for two full days per week for instruction in the industry or vocation of their choice.

Success in external examinations had shown a marked increase. The overall student passes had increased by 23% and the subject passes by 31%. The session had once again seen the expansion of College accommodation and equipment facilities, the most important of which was the building of an annex to the Wilson Institute which had added a new instructional restaurant and dual purpose classroom to the resources of the Department of Building and Catering.

Principal Liddle discussed various aspects of the corporate life of the College and made special references to the celebration in the College on the 31st May that year of the 150th anniversary of the birth of the founder, George Lauder, referred to by Liddle as the sesquicentenary celebrations. The climax to this event had been the unveiling of the huge portrait painted in oils by Charles H Mackie, which had previously hung in Carnegie's home in Skibo Castle. The portrait was gifted to the College by Mrs Margaret Carnegie Miller, daughter of Andrew Carnegie, and the unveiling had been attended by three of Lauder's descendants, Mrs Gene Tunney, Lauder's great grand-daughter and wife of the former heavyweight boxing champion of the world, Dr George Lauder Greenway, her cousin, and Mrs Tunney's son John Varick Tunney, who was a congressman representing the 39th District of Southern California. Also in attendance was Lord Migdale (son-in-law of Mrs Carnegie Miller) Miss Louise Thomson, Lord Migdale's daughter, who unveiled the portrait, as well as many eminent educationalists and public figures.

During the ceremony, John Tunney presented the College with a flag which had flown over the Capitol in Washington. A telegram of good wishes from Mrs Carnegie Miller, who was in America and unable to attend, was read out to the guests by Ex-Provost John Allan. Mr Allan then added that, even although the College was to get a new building on a new site, Lauder Technical College would forever remain as a tribute to a great man.

Another tribute to George Lauder and his ancestors was the rendering of a Lauder College song composed specially for the occasion by the College Principal Mr Stewart Liddle and sung at the close of the proceedings by the 'College Staff Quartet and Student Chorus'. The song was dedicated to the memory of founders George Lauder and Andrew Carnegie and received a warm response from everyone.

# The Lauder College Song

by Stewart Liddle

*ROCK AND TOW'R of Malcolm Canmore,*
*Dunfermline Town proclaim;*
*a TORCH UPHELD a Seat of Learning heralds;*
*a GRYPHON next declares a Name.*
*it is the Lauder Technical College,*
*TAK' TENT, BRIZ YONT, PIT TIL'T*

*two great sons of Fife and Scotland -*
*its FOUNDERS - point the way -*
*GEORGE LAUDER showed how education could be*
*geared to Work, Life, Humanity;*
*ANDREW CARNEGIE, pupil transcendent,*
*TUIK TENT, BRIZZED YONT, PIT TIL'T.*

*we who are STUDENTS of the College,*
*salute THOSE GONE BEFORE;*
*thank all the FRIENDS who help us or instruct us;*
*urge SUCCESSORS evermore,*
*cherish the LAUDER TECHNICAL COLLEGE*
*TAK' TENT, BRIZ YONT, PIT TIL'T.*

In conclusion, Principal Liddle had a prepared analysis of statistics for the session which showed that of the 444 full-time students, 12 were apprentices, 208 pre-vocational and 224 industrial. Day-release students numbered 692, 206 coming from school and 486 from industry, and evening students totalled 1616, 918 being vocational and 698 non-vocational.

In May 1966 the mystery and uncertainty of the whereabouts of a gold key, which had been used to open the first large extension of Lauder College in 1910, was solved when Dr John R Burt of New Row, Dunfermline, responded to an appeal through the local press by Principal Liddle as to the whereabouts of this important link with the College's past. It was found to have been in a display cabinet in Dr Burt's home - a stone's throw away from the College! Andrew Burt, an uncle of Dr Burt's father, was a solicitor and banker in Dunfermline and on his death the key remained within his family. He had eight children and the key was given to Dr Burt by Mrs Nan Forrester, one of his daughters, following the death of her sister, Eliza, the last surviving member of the family resident in Dunfermline. It came into his possession about 1950 and it represented to him a tangible link with Dunfermline.

In 1967 there was a general improvement in Fife's employment situation which, though good news for Fifers, reflected itself in a drop of nearly 40% in industrial full time courses for those unemployed on leaving school. However, as Mr Liddle pointed out when reporting on progress, 3,500 students had attended during the session 1966-67, and that totalled nearly 450,000 student hours, a record for the College.

Although the main part of Lauder's work had been educational, part of the work had also been industrial training and they were now making a charge on firms who were sending their apprentices to classes. Income from this had reached £5,000 in the previous season.

Mr Liddle said that once again the College students had given a good account of themselves, even on the sports field. Singling out the inter-College cross-country race he said that Lauder had scooped the pool the previous year and that despite other Colleges achievements, Lauder had again won the team championship.

The College crest: The badge depicts:
The Canmore Tower of Dunfermline; The Torch of Learning; The Gryphon – Crest of the Lauders; The Hammer and Open Book denoting the practical and theoretical aspects of Technical Education; A to Z representing the comprehensive and polytechnical character of the College.
The motto: Tak Tent – Take Heed; Briz Yont – Press On.

Staff of Lauder College during the final years of the old Technical School in Priory Lane. Taken in 1970.
Front row (from left to right): W Herdman, T Allan, ?, M I Andrews, W S Liddle, J Mason, T Allan, H Brady, I Russell
Second row: J Meiklejohn, L Arbury, A McCreary, D Henderson, E Philp, B Dalrymple, E Porter, G Smith, A Adam,
A Steedman, ? Third/Fourth row: A McIvor, J Venters, E Hushmann, J Haddow, J Yates, ?, ?, J McCann, ?, B Webster,
W Lyall, J Armstrong, T Heeps, G Metcalf. Fifth/Sixth row: J Ritchie, W Dalrymple, J Miller, ?, I Bell, ?, J Binning, ?

Eager students of Lauder's popular motor vehicle and engineering course circa 1960.

A rare glimpse of the weaving room inside the old Lauder Technical College at Priory Lane 1960. Here we see some students learning the craft.

Apprentices of Lauder Technical College in 1960 learning the art and skills of the loom.

The swinging sixties symbolised a period of great change in the country and none more so than in the Lauder Technical College which was now booming with new students. Here, Principal Liddle awards one of them the well deserved Student of the Year Award (circa 1960).

"It is 72 years ago since I was first taught in my father's snuff mill at the bottom of Hunt's Glen the use of saw and chisel of brace and bit. I always look back with satisfaction on having been taught thus early the use of my hands" said George Lauder at the opening of Lauder Technical School in October 1899.

One hundred years on and the practical skills and vision of Lauder still live on.

## POST OFFICE TELEGRAM

Charges to pay ___ s. ___ d.
RECEIVED

Prefix. Time handed in. Office of Origin and Service Instructions. Words.

OFFICE STAMP

✝TASTA TAS 602 B BPA200

At ___ m
From ___
By ___

At ___ m

SOUTHPORT CONN 61 28 1245P VIA WESTERN

LT PRINCIPAL W STEWART =

LIDDLE LAUDER TECHNICAL COLLEGE DUNFERMLINEFIFE

== EVERY BEST WISH TO LAUDER TECHNICAL COLLEGE
ON THE COMMEMORATION OF THE SESQUITENARY OF
GEORGE LAUDER WHOSE HONORED NAME YOU BEAR HIS
FRESH AND PROGRESSIVE IDEAS CONTRIBUTED MUCH TO

For free repetition of doubtful words telephone "TELEGRAMS ENQUIRY" or call, with this form at office of delivery. Other enquiries should be accompanied by this form, and, if possible, the envelope.

---

## POST OFFICE TELEGRAM

Charges to pay ___ s. ___ d.
RECEIVED

Prefix. Time handed in. Office of Origin and Service Instructions. Words.

No. ___
OFFICE STAMP

At ___ m
From ___
By ___

At ___ m
To ___
By ___

THE EDUCATION OF HIS DAY WITH WARM REGARDS AND
REGRETTING THAT I CANNOT BE WITH YOU ALL ON MAY
31ST = MARGARET CARNEGIE MILLER ==

( ( 31ST ) ✝ TS 708

For free repetition of doubtful words telephone "TELEGRAMS ENQUIRY" or call, with this form at office of delivery. Other enquiries should be accompanied by this form, and, if possible, the envelope.

---

On 31 May 1965 Principal Liddle celebrated the 150th Anniversary of the birth of the founder, George Lauder, referred to by Liddle as the sesquicentenary.

A telegram from Andrew Carnegie's daughter, Margaret Carnegie Miller in 1965 displayed regret at not being able to attend the celebrations, as well as a difficulty in spelling the anniversary title.

Left to right during the unveiling of the portrait of George Lauder was Lord Migdale, Miss Louise Thomson, Mrs Gene Tunney and Congressman John Tunney. The portrait was a gift from Margaret Carnegie, daughter of Andrew Carnegie, which had hung in their Scottish home at Skibo Castle.

**CONGRESS OF THE UNITED STATES**
HOUSE OF REPRESENTATIVES
WASHINGTON, D. C.

JOHN V. TUNNEY

October 13, 1969

W. Stewart Liddle
Kinfauns
Woodmill Road
Dunfermline, Scotland

Dear Mr. Liddle:

        My sincerest thanks for your letter
of the twenty-sixth of September and the enclosed
clipping of the presentation of the torch to Lauder
Technical College.  I enjoyed my visit to Scotland
so in 1965 that I only wish that I could have returned
for the ceremony in September.

        Many thanks for your kind words of encourage-
ment and congratulations; and your thoughtfulness in
sending the clipping.

Sincerely,

JOHN V. TUNNEY

CONGRESS OF THE UNITED STATES
HOUSE OF REPRESENTATIVES
WASHINGTON, D. C.

W. Stewart Liddle
Kinfauns
Woodmill Road
Dunfermline, Scotland

A fine example of Principal Liddle's efforts to keep
Lauder College in close contact with its roots. Here, one of many letters
from the decendents of George Lauder in connection with the sesquicentenary events of 1965.

# Lauder's New Home

In 1961, a memorandum by Dr D M McIntosh, Director of Education for Fife, stated that technical education for the large Burgh of Dunfermline and surrounding areas of Fife, was housed in accommodation most of which was out of date and designed for day-school needs. Only three of the existing buildings indeed were planned specifically for vocational further education, and one of these was some 300 yards from the main building.

*"Facilities at Lauder Technical College"* said Dr McIntosh, *"must fit into a county pattern in which a degree of centralisation, particularly of the senior stages of courses, is essential if the full benefits of economies in staffing and expensive equipment are to be realised. He further added that the County Architect indicated that to provide the necessary accommodation required by Lauder, the development of a new site would work out cheaper and the final building much more acceptable."*

The meeting approved Dr McIntosh's recommendation with regard to accommodation and agreed that negotiations be opened immediately with Dunfermline Town Council for a suitable site.

The first suggested site for the new Lauder College was discussed at the monthly meeting of the Fife Education Committee in late 1961, where it was agreed to recommend building the new College at Transy at a cost of over one million pounds. However, other sites were being identified including that of Pitreavie. A minute of the School Board Sub-Committee in the early 1960s stated that Convenor Mr Alex Eadie reported on a meeting with representatives of the Scottish Education Department and Dunfermline Town Council to consider the question of a new technical College at Dunfermline and consideration was given to proposed sites at Transy and Pitreavie. The site at Pitreavie had been unacceptable to the Department because of access and objections to the Transy site had been given on the grounds of cost and limitation of further development. The meeting then considered a site in the vicinity of Fod House, a short distance beyond the eastern burgh boundary of Dunfermline on the Halbeath Road, and it was decided to recommend the building of the College on that site.

However, this site was not without its critics and Provost Mrs Jean Mackie, who had declared the Pitreavie site "ideal", and two other ex-Provosts of Dunfermline made passionate pleas that Lauder, the pioneer technical College, should remain within the burgh of Dunfermline to serve West Fife. Mr Eadie pointed out that from the point of view of geographical advantage there was no difference between Fod and Pitreavie, but that there was a better bus service to Fod, a service which would be of benefit to all of Fife and not only those on the west. A motion to delay approval was defeated by 23 votes to 12.

Mr Colin Whitlock, Plant Manager of Philips Electrical Industries' factory in Queensferry Road, told Lauder students of Engineering at their annual presentation of City and Guilds certificates for session 1965-66 that there was a demand for diversity in training to meet the needs of the new and more technical industries that were now coming into the country. He was happy to see that the Education Authorities had recognised this and had plans to provide a new technical College. Mr Whitlock went on to say that the changing pattern of industry had been quite marked over the last few years. Whereas coal mining had taken a very large proportion of craftsmen and technicians in the past, it was not demanding so many today, but around Fife there were other industries which were going to demand these same skills and abilities in the near future. *"As we have new and more technical industries, the more vital becomes the role of Lauder Technical College".* He continued: *"It is upon such an establishment as Lauder that industries rely to provide a sound basis of knowledge for their future employees. When Lauder College move to their new premises there was the promise of a wider range of studies and this would be to the advantage of the whole community in general."*

In spite of plans to relocate Lauder Technical College to new premises at Fod in September 1966, Lauder opened a new £20,000 mechanical engineering workshop. At the opening Mr Alex Devlin, Convenor of Fife Education Committee, began by explaining the delay in the start of the new £1 million Lauder College building. *"The simple reason was that there had been difficulties, which had not been foreseen about the acquiring of the ground on which the building is to be placed. Most of these difficulties have now been overcome, and we expect a start to be made soon".* Speaking of the new extension, Mr Devlin said there was now no reason why courses could not be tailored-made to fit almost any section of industry. *"It was now important to find student sources other than apprenticeships"* he said. These newly equipped and re-situated workshops, much of which had been recommended by people from industry, now doubled the student capacity for mechanical engineering classes.

In a letter to HM Inspector in 1966 from Dr Edmund A Ewan, Assistant Director of Education for Fife County Council Education Department, following a visit to Cowdenbeath Technical College and discussions with Principal Morris, comments regarding the facilities of the College were made which became the beginning of the end for the Cowdenbeath Technical College. Mr Ewan suggested that when accommodation became available at Kirkcaldy Technical College and when the new Lauder Technical College was built in Central Fife he would be seeking to transfer the following courses from Cowdenbeath: Higher National Diploma and Certificate in Mining, HNC Mine Surveying and HNC in Electrical and Mechanical Engineering.

Serious objections to the retaining of the name "Lauder" for the new technical College in central Fife were voiced by Bailie John Simpson at a meeting of Fife Education Committee in January 1967. He had said that as far as he was aware the name of the College was to have been the West Fife Technical College and urged that this should be the name, especially in view of the fact that the new College was due to incorporate Cowdenbeath Technical College.

Ex-Provost John Allan was sorry that Bailie Simpson resented the retention of the name Lauder Technical College. The new College was neither in Cowdenbeath nor Dunfermline but was between the two, *"so why was Cowdenbeath worried?"* He did not see why a name so long associated with technical education in Fife should be dropped. He reminded the Education Committee that Lauder Technical College was the first technical College in the County of Fife, and he hoped there would be no further objections to the perpetuation of the name.

Hon Treasurer Mrs Jean Mackie, Dunfermline, was also sorry that Bailie Simpson had raised objections. Dunfermline was not being parochial in wanting the retention of the name, for no-one had done more for further education than George Lauder. *"That is the reason why we suggest that you adopt the name of 'Lauder' for the new College"* she said. The Committee approved the continuation of the name 'Lauder' for the new College by 16 votes to 6.

Staggering increases in estimated costs for new school projects led to the

Scottish Education Department calling for restrictions of expenditure which in turn led to a revision of the Fife Education Authorities 1967-70 school building programme. Fears for Lauder's new College were calmed when word came through that there would be no delay in the implementation of comprehensive education in the Dunfermline area as a result of the "cuts" in the three-year plans. However, fears of Colleges competing to provide the best courses were expressed at a further meeting of Fife Education Committee, but an assurance was given by the Committee Convenor that there would be the fullest co-operation between the different Colleges. Convenor A Devlin said that it was desirable that each College would want to offer as wide a range as possible, but at the end of the day, there would have to be some rationalisation and centralisation of courses.

Like many areas around Fife, Halbeath was once home to numerous coal mining activities as well as agriculture. Here we see another view of Halbeath in the 1920s. (DPL LHC)

The first sod for the new Lauder Technical College was cut on the site at Halbeath in May 1968. 1970 was the expected date of completion for the first "institute" in the phased development which would ultimately replace the existing Lauder and Cowdenbeath Technical Colleges. For some time huge excavating machines were seen ploughing their way through the ground on the east side of 'Fod House', Fife Pre-Nursing College, preparing the site for the new College.

The building was designed by the County Architect Department and was to be built using the County Council's Direct Labour Department. The College was planned on the "institute" principle to allow for extended development to meet future demands for technical and further education in Fife. There were three "institutes" on the drawing board for the new College, the second phase was planned for mid-1969, with early 1971 as the year earmarked for the completion.

The "institute" principle was seen as allowing the Education Authorities to build "on demand" and to integrate additional institutes into the College framework. However, the new Principal of Lauder Technical College, Mr Ian Andrews, thought that the method of building the new College, named the "institute principle" was "tactically unfortunate" and that progress at the Fod site had been limited to the first of what was ultimately intended to be a complete replacement for all the activities conducted on the present widespread scale.

Explaining the decision to amalgamate the two Colleges at Dunfermline and Cowdenbeath under the title of Lauder Technical College, Mr Andrews told Dunfermline Business Club that there had been a certain overlap between the two institutions. There was also common to the two, the fact that, while the original endowment was satisfactory for the purposes for which it was built, the passage of years and the tremendous expansion which had taken place had made the buildings inadequate and unsuited to the specialised nature of the technical and commercial education which they sought to provide. *"At the time of the decision to amalgamate, there was also taken the opportunity to experiment"* said Mr Andrews, *"In the past no sooner had a College been built than there was a request for an extension, and perhaps this was impossible having regard to site considerations."*

Describing the ever-changing climate in further education Mr Andrews said there was a changing pattern nationally and locally with the run-down of certain traditional industries. They had suddenly with them the impact of the Industrial Training Act, the different boards each producing a different demand on the further education service, making it difficult to confidently predict the requirement in any particular field at any particular time. *"I am conscious of this tremendous pace which is the keynote of things to-day"* said Mr Andrews.

Other aspects of local activity, some of which would have important bearings on the future of Lauder College, were also taking place in the late nineteen sixties. An Admiralty decision was made to close all Royal Dockyard Colleges and transfer the educational provision for apprentices to the local education authorities. This decision coincided with the completion of the new Lauder Engineering Institute and the rundown of the National Local Board training and education programmes provided by the College.

At this time there was an annual intake of some 250 technician and craft apprentices into Rosyth Dockyard, most of whom studied appropriate courses on a day release basis at Lauder. The College staffing complement was augmented by staff from the Dockyard College.

The first Institute (Engineering) was scheduled for completion in August 1970 and it was expected that this would allow the closure of Lochgelly East School in Station Road, Lochgelly and the old St Columbas School annexes. With a view to reducing further the scatter of buildings, the possibility of closing the Cowdenbeath Technical College in August 1971 by transferring the commerce and retail courses to the old Lauder building, was also under consideration.

Lauder's new College at Halbeath opened its doors to the first group of students on Monday 24 August 1970. However, the Principal of the College Mr Ian Andrews now had the daunting task of running three widely separated units at Dunfermline, Cowdenbeath and Halbeath.

Meanwhile prompt action by a welding teacher at Lauder helped to prevent an explosion in a workshop one Friday in February 1970. Mr Harry Brown and fourteen electrical apprentices were using oxy-acetylene equipment in the welding shop when the safety valve on one of the cylinders blew off and was ignited by sparks and flames from the welding. After clearing the apprentices from the workshop, Mr Brown raised the alarm and began to fight the blaze with about a dozen portable extinguishers until three units of the Dunfermline Fire Brigade arrived. Mr Brown sustained shock and a burn to his wrist and damage to his clothing. Principal Mr Andrews praised the teacher for his prompt action and courage.

At a prize-giving ceremony in 1970 County Councillor George Sharp, Convenor of Fife Finance Committee, speaking of people's skills and talents, said: *"It would be a tragedy if, because of economic circumstances, these talents were not allowed to develop. We are living in an industrial economic situation, dedicated to rapid change, and I can see no reason why facilities, costly and often in advance of those found in industry, cannot be utilised for the retraining of workers whose skills have become redundant through the progress of new technology."* He commended the work of the College taking into consideration that they had been operating, not in a self-contained unit, but in six centres.

The new College opened its doors to the first group of students on Monday 24th August 1970. Although the long and imposing footage of the new Lauder Technical College at Halbeath looked to the Dunfermline – Crossgates Road, the main entrance was in a link block on the west side of the building. The link block not only contained the main entrance to the College but also housed the administration offices. The new College was in three sections and had a paved courtyard at the main entrance. The Principal of the College, Mr Ian Andrews, now had the daunting task of running with smooth efficiency, three widely separated units at Dunfermline, Cowdenbeath and Halbeath.

The curriculum for the new College embraced the following subjects: English and Liberal Studies, Mathematics and Mechanics, and Science, Mechanical and Electrical Technology. Students could go to Ordinary National Certificate level in Mechanical and Electrical Engineering and also to the City and Guilds Technicians Certificates in these subjects.

The new College had a roll of 90 full-time pre-apprentices and 500 day-release students, the latter showing an increase of some 150 over the intake for the previous year.

An interesting aside was the maximum use of the new College Library. In the annual Library report of 1970-71 it stated that: *"From the day the College opened the library was crowded every break period and lunch time".* It was then pointed out that until the beginning of the third term, the students had nowhere to go after their dinner in the refectory except the library. However, probably due to their enforced contact with the library, even when the temporary common room opened in April 1971, the students continued to use the Library at a "gratifying pace".

Additional new accommodation for Lauder came when Phase Two was opened on Friday 12th November 1976 by Mr Frank McElhone MP, Parliamentary Under-Secretary of State for Scotland. At a cost of £900,000, the new extension, which had been in use since August, housed courses in Building, Catering, Business Studies and Mining. The weaving shed, which had seen over sixty years of service at Lauder, had closed down in July 1972 and no provision was made for any form of textile education in the new building. This was a far cry from the early years of the College when weaving rated alongside that of mining.

The purpose of the extension was to bring all College courses under one roof. With certain exceptions, Principal Ian Andrews did achieve this aim. The Building, Commercial and Catering courses were removed from Priory Lane, Dunfermline and Mining from Cowdenbeath to the new extension. The Phase 1 building was operating at full capacity and although the official capacity was just over 1,100 there were about 2,000 students on the College roll. The new extension brought relief to students and staff alike who, until its completion, had been crammed into the Phase 1 building. One regret was that some of the existing students and some of the courses for the re-training of adults had to remain at the Priory Lane Centre. However, the College did manage to maintain an equality of facilities and standards of tuition between both centres.

In 1974 Janet Leslie, the Principal of the adjacent 'Fod-Pre-Nursing College', a gift from the McCrone family and used as a centre for nurse training, retired and the opportunity was taken to amalgamate this establishment with Lauder Technical College. The Fod House was also used as a centre for the in-service training of primary and secondary teachers and at the same time in part by Lauder College as classroom accommodation. In 1991 the Regional Educational Authority gave over the whole property to Lauder Technical College for further education and training.

Margaret Millar, former Provost of Dunfermline and Patron of Lauder College's Centenary Year, displays copies of the Programme of Events for the Centenary Year, with Principal Janet Lowe.

HM Dockyard presentation to Mr R Ferguson, Principal Emeritus of Dockyard Technical College in 1974. From left to right: William John Morris – Principal of Kirkcaldy Technical College, Ian Andrews – Principal of Lauder Technical College, Mr and Mrs Ferguson, and the Personnel Manager of HM Dockyard and his wife.

The first sod for Lauder's new College was cut on the Halbeath site in May 1968. Here we see the bones of the framework beginning to take shape and the old railway sidings and workshops on the other side of the road.

# Change: 1980-1999

For Lauder College, the period from around 1980 onwards could easily be summed up by the word 'change'. The spirit of George Lauder and Andrew Carnegie would be much in evidence as the next nineteen years brought about some of the most radical and far reaching developments ever seen in the College.

New organisation, new practices, new outlook were just some of the aspects of this new phase of Lauder College. The College was in fact responding to similar challenges to those faced by individuals and companies throughout the communities of Fife. It faced two crucial elements for change: new values and economic necessity. It was these elements which made the professionalism of Lauder College all the more vital for the economic survival of the area, more so than ever before in its ONE HUNDRED year history.

Nationally, Britain elected its first woman Prime Minister in 1979, which heralded sweeping political and economic changes for the country with a programme of privatisation and cost efficiency. Half of the nation's married women were now going out to work, the highest proportion of any European country. This represented an increase from one in five women in 1951 to 9.1 million women with jobs by 1979; though the jobs were mainly part-time and in the service sector. Redundancies in Britain were reaching 40,000 a month in the early 1980s as industry prepared to weather the worst economic depression since the war. Meanwhile, unemployment reached above the three million mark in 1982. On a local scale Lauder College was to see the appointment of its first ever woman Principal as it rose to the challenges of the eighties and thrived in the variety and diversity of the nineties.

Lauder mining student, John Evans, was not only the most outstanding student of 1981 he was also the best in the whole of Britain. John, from Glenrothes, came top in the City and Guilds examinations for coal preparation practice and received the Institute's bronze medal from Fife Regional Council Convenor Robert Gough at the College's Prize Giving Ceremony. John was also awarded the Scottish Gas Trophy as the 'outstanding student of the year'. Unfortunately, the coal industry itself received no awards three years later during the year long miners' strike of 1984, which led to the closure of all but one of Scotland's coal mines.

For the first time since it was presented to the College by the Rosyth Royal Dockyard, the trophy for painting and decorating was won in May 1984 by a woman. All the more praiseworthy because the winner, Mrs Catherine Moody, Rosyth, had her first baby only nine months earlier. At the Award Ceremony Mr G W Lockhart, Training and Development Manager for Scottish Gas, said to the students that, in spite of the recession and high unemployment figures, things would improve again. *"Courage and hope were the two main factors for the youth of today"* said Mr Lockhart.

As if to highlight the new times and changes that were taking place, in 1985 the Dunfermline Council of Voluntary Services put forward a proposal to adopt the former Lauder Technical College complex at Priory Lane to house most of the district's voluntary organisations under one roof. The old Lauder Technical School had until then been leased to the Lummus Company Ltd., as a training school and induction centre for Esso Chemicals, and over £100,000 had been spent on a part renovation of the 'listed' building. The Regional Council was now trying to decide a fate for the former Lauder School/College.

John Lisgo left Lauder College in 1986 after only three years service and was replaced by Dr Alan Brown who was appointed Principal in June 1987 and soon the College took another step forward. No longer did students have to attend as members of a class or group, they were now able to study through open learning arrangements in the Centre for Accessible Learning at Lauder at their own pace and at times of their own choosing. Over 450 students took advantage of this individually tailored approach in 1988. Tutors were provided and College facilities were available for "hands on" experience on word processors and computers.

These new services extended the excellent range of evening class provision, organised throughout the 1980s by Ian Bell, Senior Lecturer in Motor Vehicle Engineering.

One of the key drivers of the extension of Lauder's services lay in the educational revolution which took place in Scottish further education in the eighties. The National Action Plan for 16+ vocational education and training introduced a modularised curriculum for all non-advanced further education. This major curriculum redesign project was followed by the SCOTVEC Advanced Courses Development Programme, which similarly modularised all Higher National Certificate and Diploma courses. Lauder College staff embraced these changes with commitment and dedication, despite the enormous workload created by the curriculum change. The College successfully embarked on an ambitious strategy to expand its higher education (HNC/D) courses rapidly.

The provision of College services to on-site training for individual companies was extended. The College was not only able to supply the business community with what it needed but was also involved in taking a lead to anticipate future trends. Lauder kept in touch with clients by having a system of Advisory Committees whose members comprised local representatives of industry and commerce. Visitors to Lauder were able to see school-leavers learning their first skills, craftsmen upgrading their original skills, executives improving their management skills, special needs students enhancing the quality of their lives and retired people enhancing their lifestyles.

For the community the College opened its doors to everyone. To the long-term unemployed, it offered hope through coaching, counselling and practice in job application skills, including interview techniques and a range of other skills necessary to compete in the jobs market. Through a long and successful partnership with the Employment Service which began in the early eighties with the first Job Club, long-term unemployed people were successful in finding employment. The College is proud to be the lead provider of Employment Service programmes in Scotland and, by 1998, operated 7 Programme Centres across Scotland. Those who had aspirations of starting their own business attended "start-up" business courses. Others who had already started their own business attended Lauder for help with day-to-day management, mastering skills in bookkeeping, financial planning, marketing and a host of other subjects.

Since 1988 Lauder had taken services out into the Fife community as part of outreach work which aimed to identify training needs and where possible, satisfy them, along with providing access to vocational training in local venues.

It was also an important part of outreach work to build good relations with local residents and to promote the work of the College in the community. Liaising with Fife Council and Fife community groups resulted in courses in wide ranging subjects from "Healthy Eating" to "AIDS Awareness".

A first-ever joint project by Schools of Architecture and a College to design and construct a family home of the future was launched in Dunfermline in November 1988. The winning design would be built in the grounds of Lauder College by students from the Construction Section. Titled Project 2000, it was a nation-wide architectural competition organised by the Royal Incorporation of Architects in Scotland on behalf of Lauder College, whose students were to build the winning design. The brief, which was circulated to more than 200 architectural students from the six schools of architecture in Scotland, was not for a high-tech dream home straight from science fiction but for a practical usable home for a young family. The Project was sponsored by the Dunfermline Building Society (principal sponsor) and by a host of other local companies. Mr David Smith, Chief Executive of the Dunfermline Building Society and Vice Chairman of the Board of Management of Lauder College made a particular contribution to the outstanding success of the project.

Two fourth-year students from Duncan of Jordanstone College of Art in Dundee, who shared the £1,000 prize, Fiona McCall from Lanarkshire and Helen Erskine from Northern Ireland, worked on their design in their spare time, and they came top of the 52 entries.

Project 2000 got underway in June 1989 with the foundation stone being laid at the College by Nurse Susan Wighton MBE, a health worker who had been hailed as a heroine of Beirut. As a patron of the project, Susan echoed the sentiments of George Lauder more than one hundred years earlier, when she said: *"practical experience teaches you 100 times more."*

By 1989, Lauder had dropped the word "'Technical" from its name because of the changing nature of the organisation from the days when "The Tech" traditionally existed for non-advanced courses, mainly for apprentices in technical subjects. Fewer apprentices now attended Lauder College and the ages and backgrounds of the students had broadened considerably.

November 1992 saw the first full meeting of Lauder's new Shadow Board of Management which was to lead the College into a new era, when it became incorporated in April 1993. The new Board was led by Miss Avril Campbell, then a director of Margaret Hodge Staff Consultants, now Chief Executive of Ross Campbell Consultants, and included representatives from industry and commerce, public services, Lauder staff and students.

Miss Campbell, who had served for two years on the former College Council said: *"I am very pleased to have been given this opportunity. I am honoured to be involved with Lauder College; it is an exceptionally good College and has a very sound management team under Dr Brown the Principal, who is highly regarded as well as respected by his profession."* Miss Campbell added: *"My interests lie:*

· *In increasing the awareness of individuals to their full potential by achieving academic status.*
· *In encouraging an acceptance of a continuing education system in response to technological, environmental and social change; from the time a person leaves school onwards through their lifetime.*
· *In establishing strong links between secondary and further education.*
· *In encouraging better communication and involvement between education and industry; and in being able to offer a flexible curriculum, based on local as well as the wider European market forces."*

In January 1993 Lauder College prepared for one of the most radical changes in its ONE HUNDRED year history. On 1st April, 1993, the College became self-governing and independent of Fife Regional Council. The College Council was re-named the Board of Management and the College began to receive funding directly through the Scottish Office Education Department. The new Board of Management paid tribute to Fife Regional Council for its enlightened and progressive government and development of the College which had enabled the College to enter into incorporation with confidence and financial stability. In particular, the Board recognised the outstanding support and direction given to the College by Councillors Jean Mackie and William Lamb as former Chairs of the College Council.

The views of Her Majesty's Inspectorate, who carried out a full examination of Lauder College in late 1992, paid tribute to the efforts of management and staff alike. The quality of teaching and learning at Lauder College was of an exceptionally high standard, said the Inspectors. *"It can be proud of its achievements and is well placed to meet the challenges of being an incorporated College."* The Inspectorate said that overall *"Lauder College was a progressive and responsive institution making a valuable contribution to education and training in the area. Good leadership both set the tone and reflected the prevailing climate which was purposeful, professional and highly committed."*

The College now had 5000 individual students, of whom 739 were full-time.

In June 1993 Lauder was the first College to achieve the prestigious international BS5750 quality standard Part 1 (later known as ISO9001) through the Training and Quality Services, a specialist quality unit of the University of Huddersfield. Their team of auditors had completed rigorous examinations of the College's quality systems. The BS5750 quality management standard was already familiar to business and industry, but the College's achievement was unique in Scotland in the educational field. It was followed up by the award of SQMs in 1994 and the Investors in People standard in 1995. These awards together with the positive report from HM Inspectorate were further evidence of Lauder's continuing commitment to quality of service.

In June 1993 HRH the Duke of Edinburgh opened the Project 2000 House of Tomorrow, and also the new Dunfermline Conference Centre built as an addition to Fod House and the Student Residence in the west part of the campus.

Lauder College had, by 1994-95, dropped its old shield crest for a more abstract chevron emblem and became characterised by further geographical diversification, through the College's success in winning contracts outwith the main College campus. Adding to Lauder's first Employment and Enterprise premises in Coates Crescent Edinburgh, new premises were also opened in James Street, Dunfermline, and further extended work led the College into Cowdenbeath, Falkirk and Tayside. Bases in Grangemouth and the Borders were established.

1995 saw the development of a new 'Three Plus' programme which was specially designed to assist unemployed people, who had been unemployed for three years or more, get back to work. Lauder College, supported by the Employment Service Programme Development Fund, designed a tailor-made programme for this group which resulted in outstanding successes for numerous long-term unemployed people.

Another innovative development involved a partnership between the College, the Employment Service and the Army Recruitment Office. In a course reminiscent of the First World War days at the old Fife Mining School, the College offered a pilot tailored programme to 15 young people to enable them to reach the standards required for admission into the Army. Of the first group to undertake this programme, 80% successfully completed the training and were looking to take up a career in the Armed Services. By 1998, Lauder College had secured contracts to deliver the School Leavers Scheme at Glencorse Barracks and ATR Bassingbourn.

In January 1996 Lauder College witnessed another piece of history with the appointment of Ms Janet Lowe as Lauder's first ever woman Principal. She took over from Dr Alan Brown who had retired after eight years of dedicated service, in January 1996. Ms Lowe had been Dr Brown's Depute for three years before taking over the post. As Principal, her aim was to give a new sense of direction and purpose for the College as it moved into its fourth year as an incorporated organisation. The new "broom" swept clean as Ms Lowe put her aims for the College into action, creating a management structure and framework designed to enable the College to thrive in a dynamic, changing and competitive environment in the run up to the College's Centenary celebrations.

'Telematics', the term for how telecommunications are combined with computer technology to transmit and receive information in the form of sound, pictures, data or text, was being developed to create new links between the College, businesses and the community. Lauder College launched "CyberTRAIN", a telematics training service and created an internal intranet, making e-mail accessible to all staff and students. CyberTRAIN was designed to be an easy-to-use technology whereby people and businesses could use touch screens and icons to access information and a range of services. It is proving to be a pioneer development in computer-based distance learning. The Fife Teleworking Centre and e/com (providing electronic commerce and multi-media production services) were launched in 1997, a further demonstration of Lauder College's determination to assist businesses in Fife to compete in a modern economic environment.

Lauder College returned to Cowdenbeath in 1997. Through support from Fife Enterprise, the Construction Industry Training Board, the Scottish Electrical Charitable Training Trust and from the European Union in the form of ERDF funding, the College purchased a large unit at Woodend Industrial Estate, and, after an extensive refurbishment programme, was able to provide a large open workshop for Construction Skills programmes and a base for the residents of the Cowdenbeath area to access College services.

The Cowdenbeath Campus was opened by the then Shadow Chancellor of the Exchequer, Dr Gordon Brown MP, on 14th February 1997, and was the first step towards the provision of a range of College services in Cowdenbeath. The new campus could provide construction and electrical programmes as well as integrated craft training in a realistic working environment. Local people could also access community education opportunities. Dr Brown declared: *"Lauder College is not only a part of the education system of Fife, it is breaking new ground all the time."*

An undoubted example of Lauder's changing flexibility and ability to break new ground, was the first Fife-wide 'Jobs Fair' which was held at the College over a whole weekend in August 1997, and opened by Henry McLeish MP, Minister of State at the Scottish Office. Organised jointly by the Employment Service, Lauder College and Fife Enterprise and Fife Council, the Jobs Fair was a concentration of effort and information about job opportunities.

One of the assets Lauder College has been able to offer prospective incoming industries to Fife is access to highly skilled and educated students. Beyond any other asset, this skilled and educated student and potential employee, has been, and still is, the key to commercial and industrial success. In this context, numerous enterprises in Fife have depended on Lauder College to provide a useful, productive labour force through the College's wide range of vocational education and training programmes. In this respect Lauder College has played a vital role in shaping the economic success of Fife and also the hopes and aspirations of the Fife community.

The College's close involvement with the microelectronics industries is the next stage of development of the inextricable relationship between the development of the College and the economy of Fife over a one hundred year period, from agriculture and weaving, to mining, shipbuilding and defence, to electronics, the service industries and information technology.

When Hyundai Semiconductor Europe Ltd announced in 1997 their intention to locate a major Semiconductor Wafer Fabrication Facility in Dunfermline, Lauder College, as it has done for ONE HUNDRED YEARS, rose to the challenge and prepared training programmes in this exciting new industrial process. The College is proud to be contracted as Hyundai's lead training provider and looks forward to working with the company when the project resumes.

Lauder's most recent years have been characterised by partnership arrangements and alliances designed to extend and enhance opportunities for education, employment and enterprise. Through a nationally significant ground-breaking partnership with Inverkeithing High School, school pupils attend programmes offered jointly by the school and the College.

Partnerships with Napier University, Heriot-Watt University and Queen Margaret College enable College students to progress to degree level education. The Fife Skillseekers (FAST-TRAC) partnership extends education and training options for 16-18 year olds.

In July 1998, Lauder College and Babcock Rosyth Training signed a unique partnership agreement which builds on an association going back 84 years to 1914 when the "Yard" became fully active. Lauder College is proud to be a lead training provider for Rosyth Royal Dockyard and recently extended training facilities for Dockyard staff by installing an on-site telematic training facility using CyberTRAIN. Under the new agreement College engineering students receive top quality practical skills training in Babcock Rosyth Training workshops.

Funding from the European Union through the European Regional Development Fund, the European Social Fund and community initiatives has made a significant contribution to the quality of the facilities and services offered to students and clients and has enabled many students from under-represented groups in society to gain access to education and training. The College's membership of the Fife Vocational Training Partnership has been of immense value in enabling the College to identify opportunities for European support and to design and implement innovative projects.

Between innovative further education and the changing demands of industry and business in Fife, Lauder College stands in a crucial position. It is an open door for young people who realise they need skills. It is a source of theory and practical training for those who are to become the craftsmen and women of the future. It has become the partner of businesses and industry who need courses specifically designed for their employees so that they can adapt and change to meet competition. It has become the key to new jobs and new careers for those whose previous jobs have disappeared through economic change. It is the way back to work for many young mothers. It is a pathway to degree education.

Employment, enterprise, education, incorporation, industry, technology, communities, competition, services, partnerships, values, new management methods, diversification, hopes, aims and aspirations. These are just some of the words which encapsulate how change had taken place over the last twenty years as Lauder reaches its Centenary. It gives just a flavour of the way in which the College has been so consistent in its readiness to change and so dynamic in the way it has responded to the challenge of change.

This book cannot hope to cover all significant changes since the opening of Lauder in 1899. It would require years, and volumes, to do real justice to the hundreds, perhaps, thousands of changes, developments, set-backs and triumphs which have been the hallmark of Fife's first purpose built College over the past ONE HUNDRED years. However, it does serve to pay tribute to the inspiration of George Lauder and his advocacy for change without which Lauder College would not be heading for its second century with optimism and confidence.

Fiona McCall (far right) from Lanarkshire and Helen Erskine from Northern Ireland took first prize in the Project 2000 House of the future design. Fiona and Helen, who were fourth year students from Duncan of Jordanstone College of Art in Dundee, shared the £1,000 prize. It was their design that would be built by students from Lauder's Construction Section.

Dr Alan Brown; David Smith, Chief Executive of Dunfermline Building Society, (principal sponsors of Project 2000); William Lamb, chair of the College Council and FRC Councillor.

Avril Campbell, Chairman of the Board of Management; David Smith, Vice Chairman of the Board; HRH Prince Philip; Dr Alan Brown, Principal. Official Opening of Project 2000.

# Men of great measure.

This Lauder student is determined to get it right and helps to carry on a technical tradition which has lasted over one hundred years.

Fod House, a gift from the McCrone family, was once used as a centre for pre-nursing training. In 1974 the Principal of the Fod Nursing College retired and the opportunity to amalgamate the building with Lauder College was taken. The annex on the left of Fod House has now been re-developed and forms the site of the new Business Learning Centre.
(DPL – Morris Allan Archive).

# The Lauder Legacy

On January 1st 1900, as the chimes of midnight echoed down the length of the country, millions of people went joyfully crazy and countless bands played 'Auld Lang Syne' as people danced and kissed their way into the new century. They had good reason to cheer. Had not the 19th century belonged to Britain? And had not the British Empire brought peace and stability to huge areas of the world? After all Britain had been both the strongest power on the globe economically and the most stable politically. But it was also a time to reflect.

Britain was Great Britain then but how much longer would it be able to wear the crown? Where now were the giants of the Industrial Revolution? And could any wealthy and civilised nation truly rejoice and ignore the conditions of overcrowding and poverty which were only just beginning to touch middle-class consciences?

In one town in Scotland an educational fire had been lit by Mr George Lauder in an attempt to answer some of these questions. He would build a legacy which would help the Fife people to success in the next 100 turbulent years.

What then of that educational fire and the Lauder Legacy one hundred years on as the nation enters the dawn of a new Millennium?

Lauder's legacy does not, in itself, command success. Lauder's College however, still strives to honour the spirit of its founder, as:

the first purpose built College in Fife
the first College in Scotland to achieve ISO9001 (BS5750)
the first College to establish bases outside its home region
the first and only College to win a business start-up contract
the first College to launch a purpose built state-of-the-art Business Learning Centre
the only College in Fife with one hundred years experience of quality in education and training

This restless ingenuity of Lauder College to adapt its further education service over the past ONE HUNDRED years to the local economy and the needs of its communities has produced as many worthy graduates as it has admirers throughout the length and breadth of Scotland.

In 1997 Scottish Education and Industry Minister Brian Wilson predicted that Lauder's new £3.6 million Business Learning Centre would make a "major contribution" to the growth and support of the Fife economy well into the twenty-first century.

In a speech at the ground-breaking ceremony, Mr Wilson said:

*"I congratulate the College on its plans and investment for the future, in partnership with local business and the community. As minister for both education and industry, I wholeheartedly endorse any project where the education sector finds out what are the training and educational needs of local businesses, and then sets out to widen access, including for the disabled, to high quality College facilities and courses which are tailored to meet those needs."*

The new state-of-the-art centre, complete with hi-tech, multi-media and global telematic links, partly funded by Europe and sponsorship from the private sector, was completed in 1998 and opened by the new Minister for Business and Industry, Lord Macdonald of Tradeston. It is widely seen as making the College the premier provider of business training and support services in Scotland. The Centre is designed to reflect Lauder's transformation from a small community College into one of the most dynamic educational institutions in Scotland.

The current Principal, Janet Lowe projects Lauder as a College with a future, built on an honourable past, all ONE HUNDRED years of it since the vision of its founder George Lauder and the entrepreneurial spirit of its funder Andrew Carnegie, first built the Lauder Technical School in 1899.

At a recent business dinner, Ms Lowe said:

*"For the past 100 years we have provided education and training for the people of Fife and Scotland. For the past twelve years we have built up a reputation as the leading provider in Britain of programmes for unemployed people, in partnership with the Employment Service.*

*Over the last four years, we have created a reputation as Scotland's most enterprising College, committed to the growth and performance of our business through working to support other businesses."*

The focus of Lauder College as it enters its ONE HUNDREDTH year has shifted away from the narrow "technical" training exemplified in the early years of the Technical School. The College is now no longer just a high quality education and training establishment but is developing the broader aspects of the Lauder Legacy by offering new opportunities through its three key themes of Education, Enterprise and Employment. The excellence of this provision has seen a rise in the importance of the College as it becomes a major contributor to the local economy through the creation of jobs, equipping people to gain employment and encouraging many into self-employment.

In recent years, Lauder College has welcomed three American members of the Lauder family who have called to visit the institution founded by their ancestor.

Gene Tunney of California, visited in 1996. He is the grandson of Mrs Jean Tunney, nee Lauder, grand-daughter of George Lauder.

In 1997, one of George Lauder's family, while on his first tour to the town of Dunfermline, paid a visit to the College named after his relative. David Greenway (62) a Boston Globe journalist, stood in front of a photograph of old George Lauder, and said that he had learned a lot about his famous ancestor from his grandmother Harriet Lauder. He met the Principal, Ms Janet Lowe, and William Runciman of the Carnegie Dunfermline Trust and was presented with a framed copy of George Lauder's portrait. His grandmother had been very interested in the family history and Scottish culture and Mr Greenway was looking forward to seeing Carnegie's birthplace and finding out more about his early links with George Lauder and his life in the town.

In 1998 another surprise visitor called at the College. George Lauder, great-great-grandson of the College's founder, and his wife Lita also made their first visit to the town of Dunfermline and to Lauder College. Mr Lauder, a retired senior officer of the CIA, spoke of his pride in belonging to the Lauder/Carnegie family and gave the Principal a family tree showing all the past and current members of the family. The College is delighted that Mr and Mrs

Lauder will return for the Centenary celebrations in October 1999.

Margaret Millar, former Provost of Dunfermline and Patron of the Centenary Year, will preside over a year of celebrations in 1999, which will commemorate the history of Lauder College over a century of achievements. Her generous support for the College marks a tradition of inter-relationship between the College and the community of West Fife since 1899.

The progress of Lauder College could be said to be as much about the life and times of Andrew Carnegie, but more especially George Lauder, as it is about any social, political or economic history of Scotland. It is in the spirit, philosophies and ideals of Lauder the great educationalist which still permeate the College buildings today, that the key to many of the progressive aspects of Lauder College, as well as to further education in Scotland, lie.

If there are people in Lauder College today, staff and students alike, who do not fear change, or what is new, or that which is difficult and yet another challenge, and who do not draw back from responsibility but welcome it, then we need only look to the man whose genius made it all happen for an explanation of the thriving success of Lauder College ONE HUNDRED years on. This was, this is and this will always be, 'The Lauder Legacy'.

## The End

# Bibliography

\*   **Andrew Carnegie**
    Joseph F Wall

\*   **A Busy Week.** 1899
    Mr Andrew Cunningham Dunfermline Journal

\*   **My Own Story** 1920
    Andrew Carnegie

\*   **A History of Modern Britain** 1815 - 1981
    H L Peacock

\*    **A Mining Chronicle**:
    Annals of the Coal Mining Industry of Great Britain
    Earliest Times - 1984
    George Montgomery

\*   **A History of the Scottish People** 1560-1830
    T C Smout

\*   **A Century of the Scottish People** 1830-1950
    T C Smout

\*   **A History of The Scottish Miners**
    R Page Arnot

\*    **EIS Congress Handbook** 1906

\*   **Journal Almanac of Dunfermline** etc 1910

\*   **Stewart Liddle  Letters and Archives** 1951-1968

# Bibliography

\* **Incubus and Ideology**
The Development of Secondary Schooling in Scotland 1900-1939
H M Paterson

\* **The History of Western Education**
William Boyd & Edmund J. King

\* **Dunfermline Press**

\* **Dunfermline Journal**

\* **Chronical of the World**
Dorling Kindersley

\* **Chronical of the 20th Century**
Dorling Kindersley

\* **An Economic History of Scotland 1100-1939**
S E G Lythe & J Butt

\* **In Search of Scotland**
H Morton

\* **Fife County Council 1890-1910**
Education Committee Minutes

\* **Scottish Culture & Scottish Education** 1800-1980
W M Humes & H M Paterson

\* **Royal Dunfermline**
A Historical Guide and Pictorial Souvenir
A Reid & W Kirk

# Appendix 1: Staff

Staff of Lauder College as at 1 April 1999.

| | |
|---|---|
| James Adams | Programme Tutor |
| Val Adamson | Lecturer |
| Jacqui Allan | Programme Tutor |
| Patricia Allen | Lecturer |
| Anne Anderson | Administration Assistant |
| Corinne Anderson | Customer Services Executive |
| Sandra Archibald | Student Development Centre Co-Ordinator |
| Alison Armstrong | Lecturer |
| Sheana Ashton | Lecturer |
| Richard Baillie | Lecturer |
| Helen Balfour | Kitchen Assistant |
| Michael Barclay | Curriculum Manager |
| William Barclay | Technician |
| Patrick Barrett | Curriculum Manager |
| Kirsty Barrowman | Lecturer |
| Joan Beattie | Project Leader |
| Jack Beck | Curriculum Manager |
| Colin Bell | Lecturer |
| Michele Bell | Administration Assistant |
| Sheila Bell | Lecturer |
| Edward Bennie | Property Assistant |
| Andrew Berry | Promotion Assistant |
| Stuart Betts | Lecturer |
| Anne Beveridge | Finance Assistant |
| William Bisset | Lecturer |
| Jane Blackie | Curriculum Manager |
| Edward Blades | Lecturer |
| Lorna Blagden | Senior Finance Assistant |
| Alan Blair | Programme Tutor |
| May Blair | Project Leader |
| Pamela Boner | Administration Assistant |

| | |
|---|---|
| Denise Bower | Senior Administration Assistant |
| Don Bowman | Curriculum Manager |
| Lorna Bown | Administration Assistant |
| Ann-Marie Boyle | Learning Support Auxiliary |
| Chris Boyle | Curriculum Manager |
| Denise Brady | Skillseeker |
| Shan Brady | Lecturer |
| Alex Brannan | Technician |
| Denise Breckenridge | Lecturer |
| Ron Broatch | Lecturer |
| Judith Broderick | Student Development Centre Manager |
| Sue Brogan | Programme Tutor |
| Tanya Brooks | Lecturer |
| Alan Brown | Lecturer |
| Ann Brown | Lecturer |
| James Brown | Lecturer |
| Margaret Brown | Lecturer |
| Val Brown | Lecturer |
| Brenda Bruce | Lecturer |
| Jim Brydie | Technical Co-Ordinator |
| Sheena Brydie | Lecturer |
| Stuart Cain | Property Assistant |
| Lisa Calderwood | Lecturer |
| Stuart Callan | Lecturer |
| George Cameron | Lecturer |
| Mary Cameron | Administration Assistant |
| Paul Campbell | Technician |
| Jaki Carnegie | Director of Finance and Administration |
| Alison Cherry | Administration Assistant |
| Alison Chisholm | Library Assistant |
| Denise Christie | Lecturer |
| Linda Clark | Lecturer |
| Maeve Clark | Lecturer |
| Norman Clark | Business Development Executive |
| Nicola Clarke | IT Support Engineer |
| Alison Coghill | Lecturer |
| Alex Colgan | Programme Tutor |

| | |
|---|---|
| John Cook | Lead Property Assistant |
| Margo Cotter | Lecturer |
| Rose Cowan | Programme Tutor |
| George Cowie | Lecturer |
| Janet Cox | Development Manager |
| Edward Craig | Business Development Executive |
| Gordon Craigie | Curriculum Manager |
| Diane Crawford | Lecturer |
| Janet Crawford | Administration Assistant |
| Linda Crawford | Lecturer |
| Linda Cummings | Administration Assistant |
| Dominic J Currie | Programme Tutor |
| Anne Daly | Project Leader |
| Annabel Del Valle | Lecturer |
| Elizabeth Den Hollander | Lecturer |
| Sandy Dickson | Lecturer |
| Alan Dobson | Lecturer |
| Tom Dodds | Assistant Principal |
| Robert Doherty | Lecturer |
| Karen Dolan | Programme Tutor |
| Andrea Donnelly | Senior Administration Assistant |
| Charlene Dougal | Skillseeker |
| Ken Dougall | Lecturer |
| Allan Douglas | Project Leader |
| Janet Douglas | Visiting Lecturer |
| Michael Doyle | Lecturer |
| Joyce Duncan | Administration Assistant |
| Martin Dunk | Development Manager |
| Joanne Dunsmore | Lecturer |
| Margaret Durward | Lecturer |
| Stanley Dyer | Administration Assistant |
| John Edwards | Lecturer |
| Graham Elder | Lecturer |
| Nick Elder | Business Development Executive |
| Sorab Eliasieh | Lecturer |
| Julie Elrick | Administration Assistant |
| Stephen Evans | Lecturer |

| | |
|---|---|
| Jim Everett | Project Manager (Distributed Learning) |
| Deborah Fallas | Lecturer |
| Fiona Fernie | Lecturer |
| Caroline Findlay | Lecturer |
| Shirley Findlay | Skillseeker |
| Lorna Finlay | Lecturer |
| Kate Finlayson | Lecturer |
| Keith Flockhart | Technician |
| Brian Fojcik | Lecturer |
| Margaret Ford | Lecturer |
| May Ford | Lecturer |
| Donna Forrester | Skillseeker |
| Julia Fotheringham | Lecturer |
| Robert Fotheringham | Lecturer |
| Elizabeth Foulis | Lecturer |
| John Fraser | Lecturer |
| Clive Freeman | Lecturer |
| Jim Gairn | Project Manager |
| June Gallacher | Help Desk Operator |
| Jonathan Gant | Bursary Administrator |
| Gary Gardiner | Internet Technician |
| Stella Gardner | Lecturer |
| Pascale Gay | Development Manager |
| Paula Gaunt-Richardson | Lecturer |
| Pamela Gell | Lecturer |
| Anne Gibb | European Funding Manager |
| Moyra Gibson | Lecturer |
| Gerry Gillen | Project Leader |
| Craig Gilmour | Lecturer |
| Mary Goodwin | Finance Assistant |
| Peter Gordon | Lecturer |
| Jill Graham | Senior Finance Assistant |
| Margaret Graham | Lecturer |
| Glenn Grant | Lecturer |
| Annette Grant-Watson | Administration Assistant |
| Linda Greig | Development Manager |
| Shona Grieve | Administration Assistant |

| | |
|---|---|
| Steven Grubb | Lecturer |
| Alex Guthrie | Property Assistant |
| Bryce Haggart | Lecturer |
| Ken Haig | Finance Assistant Stores |
| Angela Hamilton | Programme Tutor |
| Colin Hancock | Programme Tutor |
| Jean Hargrave | Programme Tutor |
| Jennifer Hawkins | Administration Assistant |
| Shirley Heigh | Finance Assistant |
| Catherine Henderson | Administration Assistant |
| John Henderson | Lecturer |
| Niall Hendrie | Lecturer |
| Rosemary Henry | Finance Assistant |
| Brid Hetherington | Lecturer |
| Dorothy Hewat | Programme Tutor |
| Claire Higginson | Administration Assistant |
| John Hill | Lecturer |
| John S Hill | Development Manager |
| Michael Holness | Lecturer |
| Helen Houston | Curriculum Manager |
| Sheila Howarth | Lecturer |
| John Howie | Technical Assistant |
| Wanda Hudson | Lecturer |
| Cerys Hughes | Administration Assistant |
| Irene Hughes | Lecturer |
| Kevin Hughes | Lecturer |
| Louise Hughes | Modern Apprentice |
| Michael Hughes | Programme Tutor |
| Alison Hunter | Curriculum Manager |
| Gerry Hunter | Lecturer |
| Jim Hunter | Project Leader |
| Robina Hutton | Programme Tutor |
| Cheryl Hynd | Administration Assistant |
| Paul Hynd | Lecturer |
| Margaret Inglis | Property Assistant |
| Irene Innes | Administration Assistant |
| Tom Ireland | Lecturer |

| | |
|---|---|
| Dean James | Lecturer |
| Catriona Jamieson | Administration Assistant |
| Joan Jamieson | Lecturer |
| Michael Jannetta | Lecturer |
| Gordon Jenkins | Curriculum Manager |
| Linda Jermain | Lecturer |
| David Johnson | Lecturer |
| Jennifer Johnson | Administration Assistant |
| Alan Johnston | Lecturer/Programme Tutor |
| Amanda Jones | Programme Tutor |
| James Jones | WAN Technician |
| Susan Jones | Library Assistant |
| Roy Joughin | Lecturer |
| Michael Kellet | Lecturer |
| Norma Kelly | Programme Tutor |
| Fiona Kennedy | Catering Assistant |
| Joe Kenny | Lecturer |
| Bill Kerr | Purchasing Officer |
| Lindsey Kidd | Business Development Executive |
| James King | Lecturer |
| Harry Kinloch | Property Assistant |
| Dawn Kirby | Senior Administration Assistant |
| John Knowles | Lecturer |
| Andrew Kowalczyk | Lecturer |
| Martin Laidlaw | Centre Manager |
| Patricia Lang | Administration Assistant |
| Christel Law | Development Manager |
| Mary Law | Lecturer |
| Douglas Lees | Lecturer |
| Annette Leitch | Programme Tutor |
| Annette Lessels | Finance Assistant |
| Brian Lister | Depute Principal |
| Alice Little | Lecturer |
| Sarah Littlewood | Programme Tutor |
| Dean Lloyd | Modern Apprentice |
| Derek Lowe | Labourer |
| Janet Lowe | Principal |

| | |
|---|---|
| June Lyall | Lecturer |
| Alex Lyle | Technical Assistant |
| John Macarthur | Lecturer |
| Simon Macauley | Technician |
| Lisa MacDonald | Administration Assistant |
| Michelle Machray | Modern Apprentice |
| Don Mackenzie | Assistant Principal |
| Birgit Maclachlan | Lecturer |
| Ross Macleod | Telematics Development Executive |
| Jeanette Mahon | Administration Assistant |
| Andrew Main | Lecturer |
| Barbara Malcolm | Lecturer |
| Susan Malcolm | Administration Assistant |
| Brian Mankelow | Property Assistant |
| Stuart Martin | Technician |
| Christine McAlpine | Lecturer |
| Angela McAndrew | Programme Tutor |
| Gillian McArthur | Lecturer |
| Sue McCanny | Lecturer |
| Terry McCrossan | Lecturer |
| Ewan McCubbin | Library Resources Co-Ordinator |
| Alex McCue | Programme Tutor |
| Iain McDonald | Multi-Media Developer |
| Stuart McDowall | Senior Administration Assistant |
| Pauline McGarry | Finance Assistant |
| Ruth McGovern | Administrator |
| William McIlwraith | Lecturer |
| Anne McInally | Lecturer |
| Angus McIvor | Lecturer |
| Donald McInnes | Business Development Executive |
| Margaret McInnes | Project Leader |
| Marjory McIntosh | Secretary/Lecturer |
| Lisa McIntyre | Personnel Executive |
| Isobel McKay | Lecturer |
| Victoria McKay | Information Assistant |
| Evelyn McKenzie | Information Assistant |
| Karen McKenzie | Senior Personnel Assistant |

| | |
|---|---|
| Sharron McKenzie | Switchboard Operator |
| Dorothy McKeon | Project Leader |
| Frances McLaughlin | Library Assistant |
| Robert McLellan | Lecturer |
| Stuart McLay | Modern Apprentice |
| Geraldine McLuckie | Staff Development Co-Ordinator/Lecturer |
| Helen McLure | Administration Assistant |
| Patricia Meach | Learning Support Auxiliary |
| Elaine Miles-Maclean | Marketing Executive |
| Irene Millar | Lecturer |
| Margaret Millar | Business Development Executive |
| Chris Miller | Programme Tutor |
| Robert Miller | Lecturer |
| Malcolm Mills | Property Executive |
| Sandra Mills | Lecturer |
| Sheena Minto | Technician |
| Audrey Mitchell | Senior Finance Assistant |
| Bruce Mitchell | Lecturer |
| Kay Mitchell | Curriculum Manager |
| Helen Moffit | Lecturer |
| Ann Montgomery | Lecturer |
| Irene Motion | Lecturer |
| Elizabeth Moyes | Senior Finance Assistant |
| Margaret Munckton | Curriculum Manager |
| Bill Mundy | Network Technician |
| Anne Murray | Programme Tutor |
| Martin Murray | Technician |
| David Newman | Lecturer |
| Gary Niven | Skillseeker |
| Jane Norman | Finance Assistant |

| | |
|---|---|
| Donald Northwood | Programme Tutor |
| Steven O'Brien | Lecturer |
| John O'Connor | Lecturer |
| Rye Ogura | Lecturer |
| Donna Orrock | Lecturer |
| Michael Owens | Technician |
| Johan Parry | Curriculum Manager |
| Janice Paterson | Administration Assistant |
| Sam Paxton | Property Assistant |
| Margaret Pearson | Lecturer |
| Elizabeth Pettigrew | Lecturer |
| Marianne Philp | Personal Assistant to the Principal |
| Sue Pinder | Assistant Principal |
| Bryan Poole | Lecturer |
| Mireille Pouget | Lecturer |
| Sarah Powesland | Lecturer |
| Paul Powrie | Curriculum Manager |
| James Prattis | Programme Tutor |
| Fiona Priestley | Technician/Lecturer |
| Ann Pulham | Lecturer |
| June Ramage | Customer Services Officer |
| Ian Ramsay | Lecturer |
| James Rankin | Lecturer |
| David Redpath | Lecturer |
| Agnes Reid | Lecturer |
| David Reid | Lecturer |
| John Reid | Lecturer |
| Morag Reid | Lecturer |
| Susan Reid | Senior Administration Assistant |
| Robert Reynolds | Enterprise Manager |
| Frances Rhodes | Lecturer |
| Lorna Rice | Lecturer |
| Nancy Rice | Lecturer |
| Renee Riddell | Centre Manager |
| Douglas Robertson | Management Accounts Executive |
| Sue Robinson | Centre Manager |
| David Roger | Lecturer |

| | |
|---|---|
| Ryan Ross | Modern Apprentice |
| Gillian Rudkin | Administration Assistant |
| Alan Scott | Printroom Operator |
| Anona Scott | Lecturer |
| Carol Scott | Business Advisor |
| Ewan Scott | Lecturer |
| Marion Scott | Lecturer |
| Russell Scott | Administration Manager |
| Mark Shanks | Lecturer |
| Linda Sharpe | Business Advisor |
| Catherine Shaw | Lecturer |
| Yvonne Shaw | Development Manager |
| David Shepherd | Lecturer |
| Archibald Simpson | Lecturer |
| Neil Simpson | Development Manager |
| Ann Sinclair | Student Records Executive |
| Beverly Sinclair | Administration Assistant |
| Elizabeth Sinclair | Programme Tutor |
| Angela Sked | Lecturer |
| Jackie Sneddon | Lecturer |
| Linda Soutar | Lecturer |
| William Spalding | Lecturer |
| Tom Spark | Programme Tutor |
| David Spence | Curriculum Manager |
| Alex Steedman | Curriculum Manager |
| Linda Steedman | IT Manager |
| Jill Stevenson | Programme Tutor |
| Alison Stewart | Skillseeker |
| Derek Stewart | Curriculum Manager |
| Gail Stewart | Administration Assistant |
| Iain Stewart | Programme Tutor |
| Ruth Stewart | Lecturer |
| Nancy Sutherland-Brown | Lecturer |
| Susan Tang | Lecturer |
| Shirley Telfer | Modern Apprentice |
| Diane Templeton | Lecturer |
| Caroline Thomson | Administration Assistant |

| | |
|---|---|
| James Thomson | Technician |
| Jan Thomson | Lecturer |
| Suzanne Thomson | Administration Assistant |
| Donna Thornton | Lecturer |
| James Tierney | Lecturer |
| Stephen Tillier | Programme Tutor |
| Helen Torrance | Centre Manager |
| Morris Torrance | Programme Tutor |
| Paul Trainer | Research and Development Executive |
| Kim Tree | Lecturer |
| Anne Tremble | Lecturer |
| Colin Tremble | Lecturer |
| Geri Turner | Relief Programme Tutor |
| Mary Wallace | Lecturer |
| Brian Walls | Labourer |
| Angela Wands | Programme Tutor |
| Fraser Watson | Technical Assistant |
| Margaret Watson | Lecturer |
| Graham Watt | Lecturer |
| Lin Weatherhogg | Lecturer |
| Helen Welsh | Curriculum Manager |
| Sarah Wheadon | Administration Assistant |
| Bruce Whyte | Multi-Media Technician |
| Mary Williams | Curriculum Manager |
| Donna Wilson | Skillseeker |
| Gary Wilson | Lecturer |
| Ritchie Wilson | Programme Tutor |
| Susan Wilson | Information Assistant |
| Wilma Wishart | Lecturer |
| Jane Wood | Programme Tutor |
| Gaynor Yuill | Information Assistant |

# Staff of Enterprise Lauder Limited as at 1 April 1999.

Pamela Bald — Financial Controller
Karen Boak — Telesales/Customer Care Representative
Cameron Campbell — Head Chef
Felia Giovannangeli — Conference Porter
Joyce Gordon — Events Organiser
Tina Lindsay — Waitress
Sonia Mallan — Telesales/Customer Care Representative
Sharon Munro — Kitchen Porter
Lauren Murphy — Modern Apprentice
Lorraine Spence — Waitress
Derek Stewart — General Manager
Daemon Taylor — Sous Chef
Sandy Thompson — Conference Porter
Gary Wilson — Deputy Manager

# *Appendix 2: The Board of Management*

Members of the Board of Management of Lauder College
as at 1 January 1999

Mr Alan Condie
(Chairman)
Condie & Co

Mr Robin Watson
(Vice Chairman)
Watson Burnett Design Partnership

Mr David Batty
Babcock Facilities Management Ltd

Ms Lorna Bown
Support Staff Representative, Lauder College

Mr Derek Butcher
Knockhill Racing Circuit Limited

Mr Alan Drugan
Student President, Lauder College

Mr Robert Fraser
NCR

Councillor Helen Law
Fife Council

Ms Janet Lowe
Principal, Lauder College

Mrs Mary Mair
Queen Margaret Hospital NHS Trust

Dr Austin Reid
Queen Margaret College

Mr Lindsay A Roy
Inverkeithing High School

Mr Iain Scott
Fife Enterprise

Mr Bruce T Stewart
Stewarts Property & Business Lawyers

Mr Graham Watt
Academic Staff Representative, Lauder College

The Senior Management Team 1996 - 1999. From left to right:
Jaki Carnegie; Don Mackenzie; Brian Lister (standing); Janet Lowe; Sue Pinder; Tom Dodds.

# Appendix 3: Lauder College and Partners

On 1 January 1999 partnership agreements were in place with:

Inverkeithing High School
Babcock Rosyth Training
Fife Enterprise (FAST-TRAC)
Napier University
Queen Margaret College
Heriot-Watt University
Queen Margaret Hospital NHS Trust
Mines Rescue Service
Fife Council
(through the Fife Vocational Education and Training Strategy Group)

The College is proud to work as partner and major training provider with:

The Employment Service
Bull Information Systems
The British Army
Hyundai Semiconductor Europe
Fife Enterprise
Forth Valley Enterprise
Lothian and Edinburgh Enterprise Limited
Scottish Borders Enterprise
Lexmark International
Dunfermline Athletic Football Club
Baxi Heating
Construction Industry Training Board

and many other companies and organisations in Fife and Scotland.

Murray Easton, Managing Director of Babcock Rosyth Defence Ltd, and Principal Janet Lowe sign a Partnership Agreement in July 1998 in the presence of members of staff of Lauder College and members of staff of Babcock Rosyth Training.

# Appendix 4: European Funding

Examples of major projects which have benefited from support from the European Union through the European Regional Development Fund, European Social Fund and Community Initiatives.

The Business Learning Centre
CALL (Phases 1 to 4)
Cowdenbeath Campus at Woodend Industrial Estate
New Engineering Facilities
SQA Centre
eïcom
Business Training Networks
Training and Sustainable Development
Opportunities in Environmental Business
Youthstart (in partnership with Fife Enterprise)
Telematics Learning Resource
Skills for Inward Investors
Telematics for Small Enterprises
Multi-Media and New Training Packages to Support Innovation in SMEs
Workforce 2000 (Key Skills)
Child Care Provision